Editor
Jennifer Overend Prior, M.Ed.

Editorial Project Manager
Dona Herweck Rice

Editor-in-Chief
Sharon Coan, M.S. Ed.

Illustrator
Renée Christine Yates

Cover Artist
Brenda DiAntonis

Art Coordinator
Kevin Barnes

Art Director
CJae Froshay

Imaging
Alfred Lau
James Edward Grace
Rosa C. See

Product Manager
Phil Garcia

Publishers
Rachelle Cracchiolo, M.S. Ed.
Mary Dupuy Smith, M.S. Ed.

W9-CDZ-404

TRAITS
of Good Writing

Grades 5–6

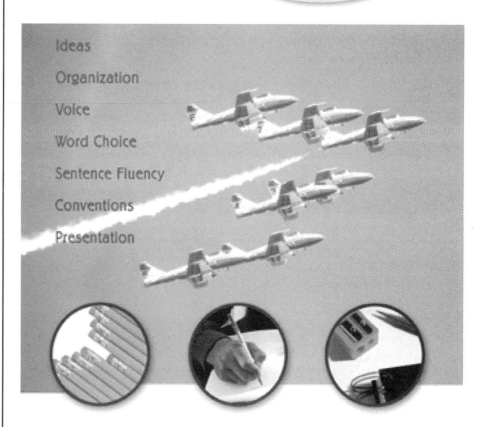

Ideas
Organization
Voice
Word Choice
Sentence Fluency
Conventions
Presentation

Author
Stephanie Macceca, M.A.

Reading passages provided by
TIME For Kids **Magazine.**

Teacher Created Materials, Inc.
6421 Industry Way
Westminster, CA 92683
www.teachercreated.com
ISBN-0-7439-3283-8
©2002 Teacher Created Materials, Inc.
Reprinted, 2005
Made in U.S.A.

Table of Contents

Introduction

If you sit down and ask teachers what good writing looks like, they will say they know good writing when they see it. But what exactly is it that teachers look for when they read their students' work? Do all teachers look for the same qualities?

In the early 1980s, teachers in the northwestern United States felt they needed a set of common guidelines by which to teach and assess student writing. By comparing student writing that needed extensive revision to student writing that did not, certain characteristics—or traits—emerged. The qualities found in successful student writing have been revised over time and are now commonly known as the traits of good writing. Recently, in keeping with current academic standards that include communication skills, teachers are paying additional attention to the way a writing project is presented. These identified traits are listed and described below.

The focus of writing centers around its message, and in the **Ideas** section, you will find activities that help students to develop their themes so their ideas are clear and easy to understand. They will also learn how to provide interesting and useful details while avoiding the obvious.

Organization is also an important element of the writing process. In this section students learn how organization provides the skeletal support for the meaning of writing. Students learn to make connections to help the reader bridge one idea to the next.

Some say that the most difficult element of writing to teach is **Voice**, but it is essential that students grasp how they can make their words come alive with the resonance of their personalities. Voice is the connection we make with the writer that makes us want to continue reading.

In the section on **Word Choice**, students will learn how to use vivid, colorful, and dynamic words to enrich their writing and make it as precise as possible. They will also learn how to avoid trite language.

Sentence Fluency focuses on sentence variety, length, and the musical quality of words when they are placed near each other. The activities help students not only to recognize the rhythm and flow of language but also to use them in their own writing.

If writing does not follow the standard form in conventions, it can be very difficult to read and understand. The section on **Conventions** focuses on spelling, grammar, paragraphing, and punctuation. The activities take the students beyond worksheet learning and are student-centered, discovery-based learning tasks.

The final section, **Presentation**, is designed to help students incorporate visual material into their writing in order to emphasize their most important ideas.

Teachers need a variety of resources to help them support students in their journey toward becoming good writers. Look in any teacher's library and you will find many, many books about teaching writing. No single method of teaching is going to be a quick solution to problems in writing, but the lessons in this book are designed to give you solid ideas around which you can effectively instruct your students.

Brainstorming

Objective

The student will generate, develop, and evaluate ideas for writing tasks using a variety of strategies.

Skills

—generating ideas by brainstorming

—adding ideas to a brainstorming list

—evaluating ideas generated

—selecting ideas from brainstorming for a specific writing task

—finding a topic that is narrow and manageable

Materials

—student copies of "It's Time to Pay the Price" (page 6)

—chalkboard or overhead projector

—writing paper

—student writing sample on page 7 (for teacher reference)

Procedure

1. Distribute student copies of "It's Time to Pay the Price." Read the article together.

2. Lead students in a brief discussion of the reasons teachers should earn a higher wage.

3. Instruct students to work in pairs to generate a list of reasons teachers should earn more money. Remind them that, at this stage of idea gathering, no ideas are bad ideas.

4. Using the chalkboard or an overhead projector, record all of the ideas generated by the students. Again, demonstrate that all ideas are good ideas by placing everything on the chalkboard or overhead projector.

5. Ask questions of the students to generate more ideas.

6. Have students organize the ideas generated by grouping similar ideas together on the chalkboard or overhead projector. Place these ideas in separate groups numbered I., II., III., etc. It is important to discuss this process at length to model for students how to effectively group ideas.

7. Once ideas are grouped, show the students that some ideas simply do not fit into the groups and should be discarded. Encourage students to evaluate the ideas generated and discard the ideas that do not fit into any of the groups.

8. Ask students to select one of the groups that they find interesting and that will give them sufficient material for writing. Chances are that no one group will be long enough to give them all the material they need, so they should brainstorm again to expand the list with specific details.

9. Encourage students to select a title for the publication based on the expanded list they have developed.

Brainstorming *(cont.)*

10. Once students are familiar with the procedure of brainstorming, allow them to work individually to brainstorm the topic of school uniforms. Follow steps 2–9.

11. Students might want to discuss the issue with students from other schools who may have different opinions or experiences. Encourage students to find other youngsters at nearby schools.

Publication

1. Have students form pairs based on the group of ideas selected. Have each pair of students create a television news story in which they present their information as an editorial. You may wish to invite the superintendent and/or the school principal to the class for the broadcast if the issue of whether or not to implement school uniforms is a current topic at school board meetings.

2. Once all students have presented their news stories, have each write a persuasive letter to the editor justifying why students should or should not wear school uniforms.

Extension

1. Send the essays to the school, local, and city newspapers for publication. Be sure to distribute issues of the newspaper to the entire class when one of the letters is published.

2. Send the essays to another school's newspaper for publication.

3. Provide students with a simulation period in which you, with permission of the parents and principal, require students to wear uniforms or to wear everyday clothes, depending on your school's uniform policy. By allowing students to experience the unknown, they will have better personal anecdotes for their own writing.

It's Time to Pay the Price

To the Editors:

I am an eighth-grade student at Fowlerville Middle School, and I am upset over the way our teachers are being treated. In my opinion, teachers perform one of the most important jobs in our community. They are entrusted with educating us and preparing us for the future. The teachers I know work very hard to do that.

We don't pay teachers enough for the very important job they are doing. The average yearly salary for educators in our area is $29,000. As professionals, teachers should be paid like other professionals in our community, such as lawyers and doctors.

Of course, the question isn't, "Why would anyone want to be a teacher?" The real question is, "How could anyone afford to be a teacher when they are paid such a salary?"

Let me tell you about my social studies teacher, Mrs. Miller. She teaches tirelessly and expertly all day. She spends her own money on certain projects for her students. She volunteers her free time on weekends to sell snacks at the football and basketball games—but she is also raising three kids. Don't you think Mrs. Miller–and other teachers like her—deserve to be rewarded for their commitment to students?

I checked with the National Education Association (NEA), and low salaries for educators is not a problem in just our area. It's happening all over the U.S. According to the NEA, teachers' salaries actually went down in 1998.

The NEA also said that in order to keep up with the growing number of students and to replace all the teachers who will be retiring, schools will need to hire over one million new teachers in the next ten years. Do school boards across the U.S. honestly believe they will be able to lure one million of the best minds if they are offering meager salaries that are in decline?

What is the solution? It is simple: Raise the salaries of teachers. Make the amount they earn more in line with other professionals.

Sincerely,

Bill Hunter
Fowlerville, Michigan

School Uniforms

You have to wear them—no choice

Like being in prison

They're ugly

They're uncomfortable

You don't have to pick out your clothes every day

Kids do better in school with them

Kids don't fight as much

They're boring because they are the same every day

Expensive—you have to buy the uniforms and regular clothes

Cheap—you don't need as many regular clothes

You don't wear out your regular clothes as fast

Ties

White shirts

Plaid

What if you can't afford one?

You don't have personality—no way to express yourself

Makes it harder to tell who is cool, who is bad

Supposed to make everyone equal, but some kids just wear special socks or shoes

Makes school safer because you can tell who belongs and who doesn't

Parents like them

Some parents can sew them

They're nicer than some of the clothes kids wear to school

Principal doesn't have to worry about dress code

Gang colors

—Michael M.

Clustering

Objective

The student will generate, select, and organize ideas for a specific writing task.

Skills

—generating ideas by clustering

—selecting ideas from clustering for a specific writing task

—organizing ideas for writing

Materials

—chalkboard

—student copies of "First Lady to the World" (page 10)

—overhead projector

—blank overhead transparencies

—wipe-off markers

—writing paper

—colored markers

—student writing sample on page 11 (for teacher reference)

Procedure

1. Begin a discussion about role models. Ask students to provide you with the qualities of a positive role model. Tell students that you are going to teach them a method for writing, like brainstorming, that will help them write more easily and powerfully. Write and circle the words *role model* on the chalkboard and ask students, "What comes to mind when you see that phrase?" It is very important to encourage all possible responses. Write the responses in circles surrounding the first and link them with lines (word web) to show the connections. Begin new clusters as ideas change. Once students have completed providing responses, be sure to point out that they have many ideas with which they can work. They only have to find the ideas.

2. Distribute copies of "First Lady to the World" to the class. Either read aloud or instruct students to read it silently.

3. After reading the article, students should work in pairs to cluster ideas about Eleanor Roosevelt on blank overhead transparencies using wipe-off markers. Instruct students to place Eleanor Roosevelt's name in the center of the cluster and to move outward with ideas about her work as a role model. Encourage them to introduce additional information about Eleanor Roosevelt if they have any.

4. Have students present their clusters to the class as you combine all of their information in one large cluster on the chalkboard. This will demonstrate the wide variety of ideas students may have and will encourage them to develop original ideas.

Clustering *(cont.)*

5. Next, circle information that could go in one paragraph because the ideas are easily grouped together. Repeat this process for the other ideas. Discuss with students the process of eliminating and organizing ideas for the purpose of writing.

6. Students should work independently at this stage as they choose role models of their own to write about. Ask them to produce a cluster of ideas about any role model of their choice. Each student should start by placing the name of the role model in the center of the cluster and move outward, writing ideas about this person as a role model. Encourage the student to provide specific evidence to support his or her ideas.

7. After students have completed their clusters, allow them time in class to share them with other students. Encourage students to add ideas to classmates' clusters.

8. At this stage, students should begin to organize their ideas to determine the information that will belong in each paragraph. Give students colored markers so that they can circle similar ideas in the same color.

Publication

Have each student write an essay about why the person selected is a role model. The student should provide a strong introduction with a minimum of two body paragraphs supporting his or her claims with specific evidence.

Extension

Allow students to share their essays in class with one another by having a read-aloud day. Make a list of the role models featured in students' essays, and after all of the reading is complete, have students select which person they feel is the most positive role model based on the evidence provided. Send the essays about the person selected to the actual role model, if possible.

First Lady to the World

When Eleanor Roosevelt journeyed to New York City after her husband's funeral in April, 1945, she greeted reporters with four words: "The story is over." She could not have been more mistaken. As the years have passed, her influence and stature have continued to grow. Today she remains a powerful inspiration to leaders in both the civil rights and women's movements.

The path to this position of power had not been easy. Born in 1884 as the only daughter of an alcoholic father and an aloof mother, Eleanor was plagued by insecurity and shyness. An early marriage in 1905 to her handsome fifth cousin once removed, Franklin Roosevelt, increased her insecurity. It also took away her one source of confidence: her work with the poor in a New York City settlement house.

But 13 years after her marriage, and after bearing six children, Eleanor resumed the search for her identity. The voyage began with a shock: the discovery in 1918 that Franklin was involved with another woman, Lucy Mercer. "I faced myself, my surroundings, my world, honestly for the first time," she said. When Franklin promised never to see Lucy again, the marriage continued. But Eleanor would no longer define herself solely in terms of her husband's wants and needs.

She turned her energies to working for the abolition of child labor, the establishment of a minimum wage, and the passage of legislation to protect workers. In the process, she discovered that she had talents—for public speaking, for organizing, for articulating social problems.

After Franklin was paralyzed by polio in 1921, her political activism became an even more vital force. She became Franklin's "eyes and ears," traveling the country after he became president in 1933 to gather the grassroots knowledge he needed to understand the people he governed.

Nowhere was Eleanor's influence greater than in civil rights. Touring the South, she was stunned to find that blacks were being denied their right to take part in government programs created to put the jobless to work. Eventually she compelled Franklin to sign a series of Executive Orders barring discrimination in various government projects.

She also challenged institutions that failed to provide equal opportunity for women. As First Lady, she held more than 300 press conferences that she restricted to women journalists. It was a clever move. She knew that news organizations would be forced to hire their first female reporters in order to have access to her.

She never let the intense criticism that she encountered silence her. "If I . . . worried about mudslinging, I would have been dead long ago." She claimed that she was not a feminist. But she insisted on her right to an identity of her own apart from her husband and her family. She was able to turn her vulnerabilities—her constant struggle against depression and insecurity—into strengths. By the time of her death in 1962, she had become one of the 20th century's most powerful and effective advocates for social justice everywhere.

Word Web

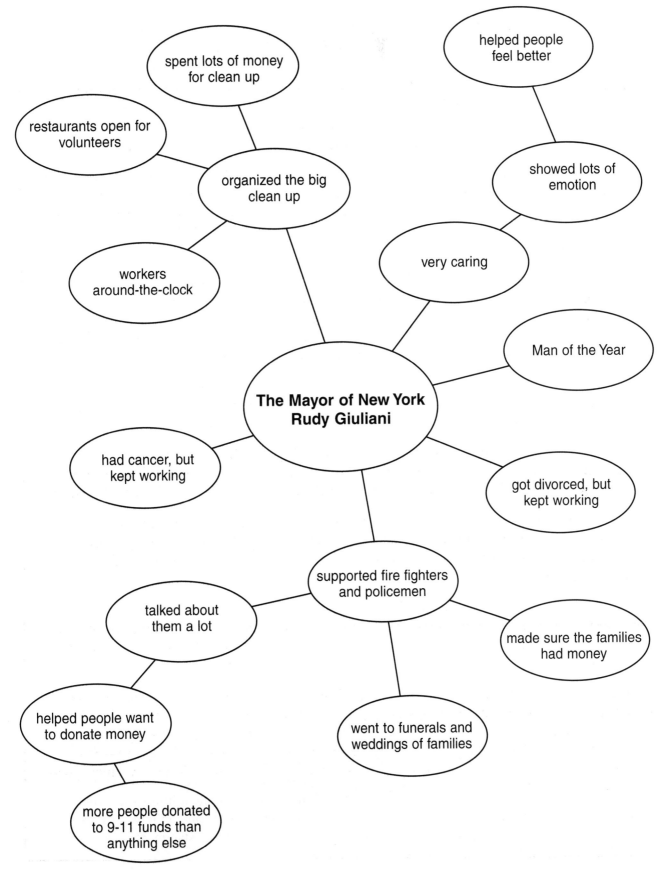

Theme

Objective

The student will identify and assess main ideas, concepts, themes, and evidence in order to generate a thesis and theme for a multiple-paragraph composition.

Skills

—discerning main ideas and concepts presented in texts, identifying and assessing evidence that supports those ideas

—generating appropriate theses or themes for essays that are neither too narrow nor too vague

—creating multiple-paragraph compositions that establish a topic, important ideas, or events in sequence or chronological order

Materials

—student copies of "Education Will Solve Many of Our Problems" (page 14)

—student copies of "Finding the Thesis or Theme" (page 15)

—chalkboard

—blank paper

—pencils

—student writing sample on page 16 (for teacher reference)

Procedure

1. Begin the lesson by introducing the concept of thesis or theme to students. Define both as *the author's point or purpose*. A thesis statement is generally found in expository writing, while themes are found in narrative writing. A thesis statement presents an arguable position and cannot be a simple statement of fact nor a personal opinion with which no one can disagree. Themes and theses present only one central idea and should only be stated as a declarative sentence. They also reflect the writer's attitude toward the writing topic. Furthermore, be sure to explain that the thesis or theme of a text can provide the reader with an organizational strategy because it can set up the information to be revealed in the following paragraphs.

2. Distribute copies of "Education Will Solve Many of Our Problems" and "Finding the Thesis or Theme." Read the articles aloud to the class.

3. Have the class work together to complete the "Finding the Thesis or Theme" activity page.

4. Circulate around the classroom to check students' work to ensure their answers are correct. Be sure to discuss how to locate a theme in a text.

5. At this stage, students should have a general idea of what a theme or thesis statement is. Place an opinion that you have on the chalkboard for the class to read. For example, "I believe teachers should earn more money." Explain to the students the difference between this statement of opinion and a fact—"Teachers earn little money." (The factual statement limits the writer from progressing any further.) Also be sure to distinguish between a topic and a theme or thesis statement. (A topic is very general, such as *poverty*; a theme or thesis statement is more specific, such as *Poverty affects the education of many students.*)

Theme *(cont.)*

6. Ask students to write five "I think" or "I believe" statements on a blank piece of paper.

7. Invite students to share their statements with the class and write them on the chalkboard as they read them. As a class, evaluate the statements to make sure that they are neither too narrow nor too vague.

8. Ask students to choose one of their five statements as the best and easiest to find evidence for supporting their ideas. Have each student place this statement on a new sheet of paper in bold, clear writing.

9. Collect the papers and redistribute them among the students. Ask students to provide the evidence for the thesis or theme as they stand in front of the classroom and present their new thesis or theme. This will help students to evaluate each other's theses or themes and work to find appropriate evidence to support ideas.

10. Post the theses and themes on the bulletin board.

Publication

1. Have students write a multi-paragraph essay using one of the theses or themes presented to the class. Advise students to choose their themes carefully, based on the theses or theme that has the strongest and most convincing evidence.

2. Publish the essays in a class book and duplicate the book for students and parents.

Extension

1. Make placards of common themes on your bulletin board and invite students to find newspaper and magazine articles, poems, short stories, books, television shows, and movies that exemplify the themes. You can have students brainstorm the list, or you can create the list yourself. Post the examples on the bulletin board below the themes. This will reinforce the students' understanding of the prevalence of theme in all writing.

2. Invite students to bring their favorite children's books to class. These books should be for pre-readers or kindergartners. Use class time to read the stories and determine the themes. Ask students to think of stories with similar themes. Make a theme wall in the classroom to track the themes featured in the stories.

Education Will Solve Many of Our Problems

Dear Mr. President,

If you asked me what to do, I would tell you to improve education. Education is the most important issue of all. Education can boost the economy, prevent homelessness, help stop the spread of AIDS, and help save the environment.

Mr. President, you should spend more money on public schools. The money would help the schools buy much needed computers and Internet software. In California, schools are very crowded. To help this problem, more schools need to be built. More scholarships need to be available so students can have an opportunity to attend college.

Education is very important. If you have an education, you can obtain a job more easily than someone who doesn't. If you don't have an education, you probably won't earn a very good wage. You might become homeless or be on welfare. Having a good education could stop homelessness and boost the economy because more people would be working.

Education can help people know the facts about AIDS. With this knowledge, a person can hopefully make the right choice to avoid getting AIDS. In this way, education may save many people from contracting AIDS. The money saved could go into AIDS research.

Education can also help the environment. In schools, students will learn how important the environment is, and maybe they will work hard to save the earth from pollution. Students will be encouraged to recycle, reduce, and reuse, therefore making the world a better place.

Improving education may not solve all of America's problems, but it will certainly help. Just by improving education, America can help prevent future homelessness and raise awareness of AIDS, maybe even prevent some people from contracting this extremely deadly disease. Education can also help show us how to save our earth.

Mr. President, by improving education, you will help people have a better life in America.

Sincerely,

Maria Judnick, 11
Alex Anderson Elementary
San Jose, California

Finding the Thesis or Theme

What is the author's main point in the letter? In other words, what is the theme of the letter?

_____

_____

_____

What four main examples does the author use to support her main point? Are these the topics of the paragraphs?

1. _____

2. _____

3. _____

4. _____

In your own words, explain how the author elaborates her evidence.

_____

_____

_____

Student Writing Sample

Which is Better?

I think San Diego is prettier than Los Angeles.

1. San Diego has less smog than Los Angeles.

2. San Diego has fewer people than Los Angeles.

3. San Diego has less traffic than Los Angeles.

4. San Diego has pretty beaches and more water activities.

5. San Diego's bay is more beautiful because there is no oil drilling.

6. San Diego has the Coronado Bridge.

—*John G.* and *Amanda K.*

Organizational Outlines

Objective

The student will outline and organize ideas for a multi-paragraph expository composition.

Skills

—outlining information

—organizing ideas for multi-paragraph expository compositions

—creating multiple-paragraph compositions that establish a topic, important ideas, or events in sequence

Materials

—your class schedule of activities

— student copies of "What's for Lunch?" (page 19)

— student copies of "How to Make an Outline" (page 20)

— student copies of "Categorizing Information" (page 21)

—blank transparency

—overhead projector

—wipe-off markers

—student writing sample on page 22 (for teacher reference)

Procedure

1. To begin the lesson, refer to your class schedule of activities. Display a copy of the schedule for students to see. Explain that the schedule is a kind of an outline because it tells everyone what will be happening during the day and when it will be happening.

2. Using the traditional outline structure (Roman numerals, letters of the alphabet, and numbers) detail the class schedule for the students on the chalkboard. Your topics should be general activities such as reading, mathematics, or social studies. You will need to place sub-activities beneath them in order to detail exactly what will happen during these class periods. Using your schedule as a model will help students to bridge their previous knowledge with outlining skills.

3. Distribute student copies of "How to Make an Outline." They may wish to use this page as a reference as they work on outlining information.

4. Before students actually outline the information from a piece of writing, allow them time to practice grouping and categorizing information. Distribute student copies of "Categorizing Information" and allow them to complete it in class.

5. Review the students' work using an overhead projector and a blank transparency.

6. Distribute copies of "What's for Lunch?" and read it in class.

7. Ask students to outline the article using the standard format for outlining illustrated in "How to Make an Outline" for homework.

Organizational Outlines *(cont.)*

8. When you have collected the students' outlines, review the correct outline with the class using a blank transparency. Be sure to discuss and account for all variations in their outlines. It is important for students to grasp that not all outlines for the same material will look exactly the same.

Publication

1. Have each students write an essay in which he or she uses the outline of the class schedule in order to describe the class' activities.

2. Encourage the student to include a paragraph about an interesting activity the class does outside of the regular schedule. Parents will appreciate reading about what the children regularly do in class.

Extension

1. Invite students to publish their copies of your class' detailed schedule of activities in outline form on poster board. Display the posters around the classroom. If your schedule varies from day to day, be sure to have some students complete the alternate schedules in outline form.

2. Have students use poster board to create instructional posters about outlining. Display completed projects on the walls. Refer to them during lessons about outlining.

What's for Lunch?

Remember "mystery meat," the cafeteria specialty that tasted like shoe leather smothered in grease? The ketchup-as-a-vegetable controversy, when a U.S. official argued that ketchup was a sound substitute for carrots in school lunches?

Well, things have gotten both better and worse. Five years ago, not even one percent of American school lunch programs met national nutrition guidelines for fat, but today you can find soy burgers and even—in Marin County, California, naturally—vegetarian meals. The problem is, such foods are but options in most of the nation's 14,841 school districts. A growing trend finds cafeterias coming to resemble mall-style food courts. In Fort Collins, Colorado, kids can eat Pizza Hut, Taco Bell or McDonald's food without leaving the cafeteria. The lunchroom at Burleson (Texas) High has been transformed into the Elk City Cafes, with sandwiches, burgers, and other fare served from places like Red Rack's and Mama's Pizza Place. Nearly a third of all U.S. high schools now serve name-brand foods; in Colorado, Pepsi and Coke recently paid three school districts as much as $8.7 million each for the right to peddle their products in vending machines.

Is this a good idea in a country where kids are in worse physical condition than ever? More than seven million American children are overweight, says the National Center for Health Statistics, and childhood obesity levels are at an all-time high (a 12-year-old boy in the '90s weighs 10.5 pounds more than two decades ago). Some studies show dangerously high cholesterol levels in eight-year-olds. And you can bet that profits from the fast-food giants are not going a long way toward reinvigorating physical education programs, which were among the first cuts during the last business slowdown.

Radical remedies are needed, so let's go to a radical guy. "I'd remove junk-food vending machines from schools," say health guru Dr. Dean Ornish, who consulted on school nutrition guidelines in 1995 but who has no control over the Domino's effect now sweeping our cafeterias. "Most children have no experience of where food comes from, other than the grocery store. Know what I'd do? Plant a school garden in every school. That'll allow children to plant food, watch it grow, harvest it, prepare it, eat it." Now there's food for thought.

How to Make an Outline

An outline lets you look at a great deal of information at a glance. Outlines are easier to read than mere notes about a subject because they arrange the information on the page to show their relative importance and their connections with each other.

There is a standard format for outlines, and the indentations are used to make finding the information on the page easier for the reader. The more important the information, the closer it appears to the left margin.

Here is an outline for an assignment in language arts:

Thesis statement: a brief statement of the topic

 I. First major point

　　A. First point related to I.

　　　　1. First sub-point to explain I.A.

　　　　　　a. First sub-point to explain I.A.1.

　　　　　　b. Second sub-point to explain I.A.1.

　　　　2. Second sub-point to explain I.A.

　　B. Second point related to I.

　　　　1. First sub-point to explain I.B.

　　　　　　a. First sub-point to explain I.B.1.

　　　　　　b. Second sub-point to explain I.B.1.

　　　　2. Second sub-point to explain I.B.

 II. Second major point

　　A. First point related to II.

　　B. Second point related to II.

Categorizing Information

Can you number and arrange the following unorganized words into a logical and standard outline? Use as many main points and sub-points as you need.

I. Means of Transportation

   A. _____

      1. _____

      2. _____

      3. _____

         a. _____

   B. _____

      1. _____

         a. _____

      2. _____

   C. _____

      1. _____

         a. _____

         b. _____

   D. _____

      1. _____

      2. _____

         a. _____

I. Clothing

   A. _____

      1. _____

      2. _____

         a. _____

   B. _____

      1. _____

      2. _____

   C. _____

      1. _____

      2. _____

      3. _____

   D. _____

   E. _____

---

yachts	trains	shirts
caps	Cesnas	baseball hat
trolley	slacks	footwear
suits	flip-flops	boats
jeans	automobiles	airplanes
jets	the Titanic	sandals
cars	Ferraris	trucks
shorts	pants	sports cars
stealth bombers	sneakers	
cruise ships	bullet trains	
berets	electric trains	

Daily Schedule

I. Morning
   A. arrival to class
      1. Students come in and sit down.
      2. Mrs. H. does roll call.
         a. Buddies for absent students are reminded to collect work, take notes, and call them.
   B. opening/announcements
      1. Say the Pledge of Allegiance.
      2. Mrs. H. makes daily announcements and reviews schedule of activities for the day.
   C. math/science
      1. Review lesson from previous day.
      2. Review and collect homework.
      3. Learn new concept.
         a. Practice new skill.
         b. Start homework for new skill.
II. Mid-day
   A. independent work
      1. Students work independently in centers or read silently.
   B. P.E. and recess
      1. Students eat lunch and talk to friends.
      2. Students play sports.
III. Afternoon
   A. language arts
      1. Review lesson from day before.
      2. Review and collect homework.
      3. Learn new concept.
         a. Practice new skill.
         b. Start homework for new skill.
   B. social studies
      1. Review what we learned yesterday.
      2. Read in textbook.
      3. Mrs. H. talks to us.
      4. Do activity or have a discussion.
IV. Closing
   A. reminders for homework and activities for next day
   B. clean up
      1. Clean up around and in desks.
      2. Clean up classroom.
      3. Close windows and lock up room.
   C. dismissal

—Jack K.

Paragraph Topics

Objective
The student will develop and support a clearly stated theme for multi-paragraph expository compositions.

Skills
—develop an appropriate and clearly stated theme for a multi-paragraph expository composition
—provide details, examples, and facts in order to support a theme

Materials
—student copies of "Coping with Conflict" (page 25)
—student copies of "Convincing Details" (page 26)
—writing paper
—student writing sample on page 27 (for teacher reference)

Procedure
1. Begin the lesson by reviewing the qualities of a theme or thesis statement. (A theme is the statement of the author's purpose and usually provides a simplified version of the reasons behind the author's beliefs.)

2. Add to the students' definition of theme by pointing out that a good theme will provide the organizational structure of a piece of writing. Illustrate this by placing the following example on the chalkboard: *The city should plant more trees.*

3. Ask the students why the city should plant more trees. After they have come up with some reasons that can be argued effectively, rewrite the theme to include their reasons. For example, "The city should plant more trees because they decrease the effects of pollution, they attract wildlife to the community, and they make the city more beautiful."

4. Now the students will know what to write about in the paragraphs following the introduction. One paragraph should be devoted to each of the reasons supporting the theme. Explain that sometimes the theme and the reasons do not appear in the same sentence, but nonetheless, they should appear somewhere near the beginning of the piece of writing.

5. Distribute student copies of "Coping with Conflict." Have students read the article silently.

6. Discuss the organization of the article and the topics of each supporting paragraph. Point out that while this article does not follow the strict structure of a theme with a built-in organizational structure, it does follow an organizational pattern—problem, effect, solution. Also be sure to point out that each paragraph has one main point and that all sentences in the paragraph exist to develop the main point.

Paragraph Topics *(cont.)*

7. Once students have an understanding of supporting the theme through paragraph topics, have them apply the skills to real life. Decide in advance that you will give your students a new privilege if they can provide convincing reasons and thorough explanations to support their desire for the privilege. You may wish to allow them to choose the privilege. This will require them to negotiate and prioritize their desires.

8. Have students complete "Convincing Details" to further their arguments.

Publication

1. Have students write essays in which they attempt to convince you to allow them a new privilege. Be sure to encourage them to use convincing evidence in their paragraphs to support their main idea.

2. Publish the essays in a newsletter and send copies to parents and other classes in the school.

Extension

1. Instruct students to select other issues that are important to them and write about them, such as the need for hot water from the faucets in the school bathrooms, more nutritional lunches, longer breaks, longer recess, new trash cans, more trees and foliage on campus, more recreational reading time, etc. Encourage the students to be realistic in their requests. When essays are completed, submit them to the appropriate readers so the students will be empowered when they enact change at home, at school, or in the community.

2. Provide students with a list of topics and themes and ask them to provide you with appropriate supporting paragraph topics.

Coping with Conflict

The loudspeaker crackles in a sixth-grade classroom, and a hearty voice announces a moment of silence "in honor of our fellow students and colleagues in Colorado." The kids at Kennedy Middle School are quiet and worried. In their own hometown of Eugene, Oregon, about a year ago, Tony Case and a bunch of schoolmates lay in the E.R. fighting for life. The kids figured the nearby shooting was a one time thing, until it happened again in Littleton, Colorado. Now they recite an oath written by local schoolchildren. "I will work to be a better observer and listener, a more thoughtful friend," they chant. "I will discourage any shows of violence."

Human beings can be violent—when they learn not to be, it's called civilization. But in the U.S., both victims and offenders are getting younger. In 1998, there reportedly were close to a million assaults on teens by teens. Though lower than a few years ago, those numbers are still far higher than they were in the early 1980s. Most of the killings that involve kids do not occur in schools or in suburbs; they are urban street crimes. Tightly supervised, schools are arguably the safest places children can be.

At Kennedy three years ago, teachers were complaining that they had the worst sixth-grade class ever. The new principal, Kay Mehas, instituted a violence-prevention program called Second Step. All adults in the school, from principal to custodian, were trained to teach it. The first year, Mehas had 1,400 referrals (kids sent to the office for behavior problems) and 15 incidents involving weapons—knives, a BB gun, pins shot through a straw. Referrals were down a third the next year, while attendance and academic performance were up. This year she got an e-mail from the principal of the high school saying that her "bad" sixth-grade class had turned into his best freshman class ever.

The sixth-graders are learning empathy, going around the room talking about feelings. "I feel upset . . . ," says one, ". . . when people steal my things . . . ." ". . . I need to know that people will leave my things alone," adds another. Then comes role-playing, putting yourself in someone else's place, a skill that killers lack. Chess and checkers teach kids to control impulsive behavior. "From kindergarten on, we must teach kids to stop and think," says a school psychologist.

Some 15 percent of students everywhere say they have problems with bullies. In one Second Step class at Kennedy, the kids discussed how the shootings could have been prevented. They suggested more kindness on the part of the schoolmates, better role models, less violent television and more involved parents. Kennedy counselor Sharon Tabor believes that all adults need to help parents who are stretched too thin. "We can't do it any other way," she says. "All the kids are ours."

Convincing Details

What do you want to convince the teacher to give you as a privilege?

_____

_____

Why do you want this privilege?

_____

What are the reasons you have for believing you should have this privilege?

_____

_____

Provide details and specific examples to support your ideas.

_____

_____

_____

Anticipate your teacher's reaction to your evidence and examples. What can you use as a counter-argument?

_____

_____

_____

Student Writing Sample

Chewing Gum Should Be Okay

   Chewing gum is fun and we want being in school to be fun, too. The students in our class should be allowed to chew gum while we are in school. Chewing gum keeps us from talking too much. It also keeps us from getting too hungry. And we promise to throw our gum in the trash when we are done.

   I've noticed that when I chew gum, I don't talk to the person sitting next to me as much. I guess it is because my mouth is already busy. I know some kids who chew very loudly, like cows. Other kids chew gum even though they are not allowed to and they never get in trouble because they chew so carefully and quietly. They don't talk a lot because they don't want to get caught by the teacher.

   Besides making me more quiet, chewing gum keeps me from getting too hungry in class. I am always hungry. I could eat all day long. My dad says it is because I am growing. But when I chew gum, I eat less. Eating in class is too messy and I know Mrs. K won't let us eat in class even if we have good reasons. But chewing gum is good enough when we have to wait for lunch.

   Last year Mr. B said that we couldn't chew gum because kids leave gum under the desks instead of putting it in the trash. And he said a boy threw gum in a girl's hair one time. I think our class will be extra careful about their gum and will put it in the trash, but only when we raise our hands to get up. Kids put gum under desks when they aren't supposed to chew it and they don't want the teacher to know they have it. But if you know, they won't hide it.

   I really want to chew gum in class. Not everyday, but some times. It keeps us from talking too much and from getting hungry. We will throw our gum in the trash and not on the floor or under the desks. We promise.

—Kyle M.

Paragraph Development

Objective

The student will develop a topic and supporting paragraphs using a variety of methods.

Skills

—developing a topic with supporting evidence for a multi-paragraph essay

—developing paragraphs using a variety of methods

Materials

—a variety of articles from newspapers and magazines

—chalkboard

—student copies of "Will Teens Disappear?" (page 30)

—student copies of "Supplying Examples and Details" (page 31)

—red marker

—writing paper

—student writing sample on page 32 (for teacher reference)

Procedure

1. Explain to students that they can use a variety of methods to develop paragraphs to support their thesis statements. They can use facts, examples, details, definitions, comparison and contrast, an incident, anecdote or story, statistics, names, or sensory details to help develop their ideas in paragraphs.

2. Provide students with various articles from newspapers, magazines, or the Internet. Try to select articles that represent all or almost all of the methods for developing paragraphs. Place students in pairs or small groups and read the articles to determine if the paragraphs are developed using the methods listed above. Invite students to read their paragraphs aloud and then identify the method the author used to develop the ideas. Be sure to discuss all methods listed above, and encourage students to find methods other than those listed that are used to develop the paragraphs.

3. Place the headings on the chalkboard and be sure to provide some examples for the students to see.

4. Distribute student copies of "Will Teens Disappear?" Have the students read the article silently.

5. Ask students to work independently to identify the methods used to develop the paragraphs. Instruct them to write the method used to develop each paragraph beside it on the copy of the article. Check work for accuracy and clarify any confusion.

6. Before you distribute copies of "Supplying Examples and Details" to the students, draw a red star on five of the papers. Have the students work independently to complete the activity. Ask the students with the stars on their papers to present their sentences to the class by writing them on the chalkboard.

Paragraph Development *(cont.)*

7. Have each student write a letter to a teacher they believe is special. Help each student to develop a strong thesis statement about why this teacher is special and require him or her to develop body paragraphs using facts, examples, details, definitions, comparison and contrast, an incident, anecdote or story, statistics, names, or sensory details to help develop their ideas. Encourage the student to use the structure in "Supplying Examples and Details" in their letters.

Publication

1. Mail all of the essays to the teachers addressed.

2. To motivate the students and teachers, produce a newsletter which contains all of the essays and distribute them throughout the school.

3. Mail copies of the essays to the principals, superintendents, and/or school board members of the schools where the teachers work.

Extension

1. Create a bulletin board containing the following headings—facts, examples, details, definitions, comparison and contrast, an incident, anecdote or story, statistics, names, or senses. Invite students to find paragraphs developed using these methods and place them below the appropriate heading.

2. Each day select a student from the class to sit in the middle of a large circle. Invite the class to use facts, examples, details, definition, comparison and contrast, an incident, anecdote or story, statistics, names, or the senses to support why they believe that the particular student is special. Each day have each student write a well-developed paragraph about the selected student using the information presented in the circle. Be sure to give copies of the paragraphs to the students about which they are written. (This activity is a great community-builder as well as an exercise in developing and supporting ideas.)

3. Take the students to the library to research topics of their choice. Have them write well-developed paragraphs using facts, examples, details, definition, comparison and contrast, an incident, anecdote or story, statistics, names, or the senses to support their ideas.

Will Teens Disappear?

Of all the great post-World War II inventions—television, rock 'n' roll, the Internet—the greatest and most influential is, perhaps, the American teenager. The country has always had adolescents—human beings between the ages of 12 and 18. But it was only in the past 50 or 60 years that it had tens of millions of semi-grownups living in a buffer zone somewhere between childish innocence and adult experience.

This teenage culture of pop songs, cars and acne ointments, of proms, allowances and slumber parties is still unknown in less developed countries. And until the reform of child-labor laws in the 1930s, the spread of suburbia in the 1940s and the rise of targeted youth marketing in the '50s, it was unknown here as well. Early 20th century adolescents were farmers, apprentices, students and soldiers—perhaps even wives and husbands—but not teenagers.

How much longer will teenagers exist, at least in the form that James Dean made famous? Twenty years, tops, is my guess. Teenagers, as classically defined, are changing into something different. The buffer zone they once inhabited is being squeezed out for two reasons: children are growing up faster than ever, and adults are growing up more slowly.

Not long ago, my Internet access was restored by a 16-year-old who charges $50 an hour and trades stocks over the Web. An adolescent with his or her own money—real money, not parental charity—is not, in any meaningful sense, a teenager, but a capitalist early bird out to get the worm.

The right to be economically unproductive until the day after college graduation—amendment one to the teenage constitution—will seem downright crazy in a few years. Fourteen-year-olds in 1950 were not expected to know how to use metal lathes even if one day they might end up working for General Motors. But nowadays 14 seems rather late to learn the skills required for a position at a major software company.

The next distinction to vanish will be social. One thing that used to make teenagers teenagers was the postponement of family responsibilities. But these days even 30- and 40-year-olds are postponing family responsibilities, often permanently. Coming of age is becoming a lifelong process. Teenagerhood as preparation for life makes no sense when the life being prepared for resembles the one you've been living all along.

What will a world without teenagers look like? Like the adult world does right now. The carefree years will become the prudent years, and the prudent years will continue throughout life. Adolescents will feel the same pressures as their parents do: to succeed financially, to maintain their health, to stay on society's good side. That's how it used to be, in the 19th century, and that's how it will be again in the 21st. The age of James Dean, the Ford Mustang, and the going steady will seem, in retrospect, like what it was: a summer vacation from larger human history.

Supplying Examples and Details

Supplying Examples

When writing an essay, it is important to support each generalization with a specific example. For the topic sentence below, write three more sentences that supply examples. Also, write a concluding sentence that could sum up the paragraph.

No matter where I buy it, I love pizza.

1. _I love the extra-crunchy crust that Pizza Hut makes._
2. _____
3. _____
4. _____
5. _____

Supplying Details

It is also important to supply details to support generalizations in paragraphs. For the topic sentence below, write three details and a concluding sentence that could sum up the paragraph.

What is it about a hamburger that starts my mouth watering? Let me count the ways.

1. _____
2. _____
3. _____
4. _____

Student Writing Sample

Letter to the Teacher

Dear Mr. Nelson,

Thank you so much for being my teacher. You are really funny and really nice. You are also really smart and you are a good teacher. I love your style of teaching. You make teaching fun. I loved being in your class last year. You gave good examples and you taught us so that we could all learn it on the first try. You graded hard, but we all got good grades because you were such a good teacher. You taught me so much.

Thank you from your former student,

Alex

—Alex M.

Ordering Information

Objective

The student will write and organize paragraphs in a logical fashion presenting the information from the general to the more specific.

Skills

—writing paragraphs in which the information is presented in a logical fashion

—organizing information from the general to the more specific

Materials

—chalkboard

—overhead transparencies of model paragraphs using the general to specific structure

—overhead marker

—an overhead projector

—student copies of "Lice on the Loose!" (page 35)

—student copies of "Reordering Information" (page 36)

—a variety of newspaper and magazine headlines

—writing paper

—student writing sample on page 37 (for teacher reference)

Procedure

1. Because students are still struggling at this level with writing organized paragraphs, it is important that they understand that once they learn the basic structure of a paragraph, they can vary it or adapt it to meet their increasingly more sophisticated needs. By presenting information using the basic pattern of naming the topic, narrowing or restricting the topic, and illustrating the topic, students will have a basic structure with which to work. Once they master this technique, they can move on to using other techniques.

2. Ask students to imagine that they are going to cook a very impressive meal. First it is important to decide on a type of food to make. Choose Italian food (topic) for this activity. Now make a menu. The kind of menu will be a lunch menu (narrowing of topic). Then determine each of the dishes on the menu, such as lasagna, spaghetti, gnocchi, and escarole (illustration). Record each step on the chalkboard.

3. Provide students with examples of paragraphs using the general to specific structure. As you review the examples with the students, point out how the author names the topic, narrows or restricts the topic, and then uses an illustration.

4. Distribute copies of "Lice on the Loose!" and read the article aloud as a class. Review how the author orders the information from the general to the specific.

5. Distribute copies of "Reordering Information" to the students. Allow them to work independently and complete the activity page in class.

Ordering Information *(cont.)*

6. Have students work in pairs to review their answers.

7. Provide the students with a variety of newspaper and magazine headlines that they can write about. The headlines should deal with news stories, sports, features, human interest, the arts, cooking, and other topics.

8. Ask each student to write a paragraph about the headline using the general-to-specific pattern.

Publication

Produce a class newspaper featuring the paragraphs using the general-to-specific pattern. (It will be an enjoyable read if the headlines students selected are funny and interesting.)

Extension

1. Reproduce ten different paragraphs—some that use a general-to-specific pattern and others that do not. Ask students to identify the ones that follow the pattern.

2. Provide the students with a few good models of paragraphs following the general-to-specific pattern, but omit the topic sentence or the sentence that narrows or restricts the topic. Ask students to fill in the blank.

Lice on the Loose!

Rachel Carson Elementary School in Gaithersburg, Maryland, was invaded in 1998. To combat the intruders, school officials banned hairbrushes. Kids were ordered to place their coats in plastic bags. Five nurses were assigned to check 600 heads. Sound familiar? Yep, you guessed it. Head lice had invaded the school.

From New York to California, the human head louse is on the loose in schools. Each year, 10 million to 12 million Americans get head lice. The sesame-seed-size insects make themselves at home on human scalps and lay eggs, called nits, that they cement to strands of hair. Head lice do not carry disease, but they are a nasty—and itchy—pest.

The head louse has been annoying humans for thousands of years. Archaeologists have found signs of lice in the hair of ancient Egyptian mummies.

Modern humans use chemicals to get rid of the pests. For decades, chemical shampoos and rinses helped control head-lice outbreaks. In recent years, outbreaks have become more and more frequent. The tiny insect appears to have become harder to kill. Parents say that just days after treating their kids for lice, the itchy bugs are back.

SURVIVAL OF THE FITTEST

Thousands of parents and school officials call county health offices to report that the ordinary lice-killing products just don't seem to be working. Wayne Kramer, an insect expert for Nebraska, received 125 calls in the first four months of school. "I think it's on the brink of being out of control," he says.

Many health officials fear that a stronger kind of head louse has emerged. Scientists believe that permethrin (per-meth-rin), the main chemical used in many lice-killing products, killed off weaker lice. That would leave only the stronger lice, and permethrin just can't kill them.

This theory has yet to be proved. But families who have experienced the problem say that theory sounds about right. Says Michele Colburn, who recently spent six months battling lice on her 11-year-old daughter: "The lice would disappear from her head and then reappear. I tried every shampoo on the market, but they would just keep coming back."

A NIT-PICKING SOLUTION

What do the experts recommend? The key is the removal of the nits. Lice eggs are much harder to spot than the full-grown lice. But if the nits are not removed or combed out, the insects will reappear. So keep combing!

Reordering Information

Take the following disorganized lists of words and reorder them so that they are organized from the general to the more specific.

Pasta   _____

3 courses   _____

Food   _____

Spaghetti   _____

European Cuisine   _____

Macaroni   _____

Italian Food   _____

Gnocchi   _____

Action   _____

Bruce Willis   _____

Die Hard   _____

Entertainment   _____

Hobbies   _____

Movies   _____

Suspense   _____

Grade 5   _____

Education   _____

Elementary School   _____

Institution   _____

Primary Grades   _____

Values   _____

Student Writing Sample

Shattering the Illusions and Myths of Television and Advertising

PBS doesn't have advertising, so my parents would only let me watch PBS if I wanted to watch cartoons when I was younger. PBS doesn't have advertising because they are public television and they get their money from donations from people who watch the shows instead of from the advertisers who put on commercials. But I noticed PBS has changed the way they tell us who the sponsors of the shows are. They used to just say at the end of a show, "Sponsored in part by Cheerios," for example. But now they have a little commercial, except I noticed that they don't show the product in the commercial, they just have the logo. This is a trick. Parents think their kids don't see commercials on PBS, but they do. The commercials are just different on PBS than on regular televsion. And when my little sister was watching "Elmo's World" on Sesame Street, I noticed a lot of references to the Internet and getting e-mail. It seems like the show is selling something. My sister is too little to know what e-mail is, but Elmo sure does talk about it a lot.

—*John R.*

Transitions

Objective

The student will be able to recognize and utilize details and transitional expressions in order to link one paragraph to another in a clear line of thought.

Skills

—identify details and transitional expressions in reading material

—understand the purpose and function of transitions in writing

—utilize thoughtful transitions that clearly show how ideas connect

Materials

—overhead transparency of "A Real Pain in the Neck" (page 40)

—overhead projector

—chalkboard

—student copies of "A Handy List of Transitional Phrases" (page 41)

—student copies of "Adding Transitions" (page 42)

—student writing sample on page 43 (for teacher reference)

Procedure

1. Begin the lesson by asking students if they like wearing backpacks. This should begin a lively discussion about backpacks, books, lockers, etc.

2. Place the transparency of "A Real Pain in the Neck" on the overhead projector. Read the article as a class.

3. Point out the author's use of transitions in the article. First discuss how the author links the first two paragraphs with one sentence about Jordan being only one of many who needs to pay attention to how heavy his load is. The author uses the first sentence of the third paragraph to make sure readers can follow the switch to talking about Dr. Alexander's study, which wasn't part of the A.A.O.S. at all. The transition between the third and fourth paragraphs is not obvious, but the last sentence in paragraph three is about a 47-pound backpack, and the first sentence of paragraph 4 continues the thought with a question about how a person should carry such a heavy load. The final paragraph functions as a transition unifier. The author returns to Jordan, which helps link the previous paragraphs to the beginning of the article.

4. Begin instructing students about the importance of transitions in writing by using your own class activities as an example. Describe to the students what methods you use to switch the class from one activity to the next. Explain that when teachers fail to have smooth transitions, abruptly changing from one activity to the next, they lose students' attention because the students cannot anticipate what is going to happen next. Transitions in writing are just as important as transitions in leading groups. They help keep the reader or listener interested and focused.

Transitions *(cont.)*

5. Invite the students to brainstorm a list of all of the transitional words they can develop. Write these on the chalkboard.

6. Distribute copies of "A Handy List of Transitional Phrases" as a reference to the students. Review the list and point out when the transitional phrases would be useful in particular writing situations. For example, *moreover* is helpful when signaling an addition to previous information. Be sure to remind students that the overuse of transitional phrases can cause writing to be awkward and boring. Encourage them to use the repetition of ideas and key phrases as well.

7. Distribute copies of "Adding Transitions" for students to complete.

8. Review the activity page as a group.

Publication

1. Have students select a piece of writing they have already completed and rewrite it using effective transitions. By having students work with already completed pieces of writing, they can focus on making the transitions work most effectively and smoothly.

2. Instruct each student to complete an essay in which all paragraphs and ideas are linked using transitional phrases or repetition of ideas or key words. Require the student to underline or highlight the transitions in the final draft and have a peer-editing session in which students evaluate the effectiveness of the transitions.

Extension

1. Ask students to bring in articles from newspapers and magazines that contain good examples of transitions. Have the students use highlighter pens to draw attention to the transitions. Post the articles on your bulletin board in the classroom.

2. Provide students with stacks of magazines. Have them work in pairs to identify transitions in articles. They might work against a time limit with the winning team being the one with the most extensive list of transitions found.

3. Take a trip to the school library. Ask students to work in teams of three, requiring them to locate, identify, and present writings that contain good examples of transitions.

A Real Pain in the Neck

Kids with heavy backpacks should lighten up!

Carrying a backpack can be hazardous to your health. Just ask Jordan Morgan, 10, of California. "One time I fell off my bike and bruised my leg because my backpack was too heavy!" says Jordan. He weighs 100 pounds. His backpack, loaded with four books, a calculator, a binder, paper, glue, and gym clothes, can weigh 20 pounds! "Sometimes I have to stop and rest because it's too heavy."

Jordan isn't the only one who needs to lighten his load. In October 1999, the American Academy of Orthopedic Surgeons (A.A.O.S.) reported that thousands of kids have back, neck, and shoulder pain caused by their heavy backpacks. The A.A.O.S. surveyed more than 100 physicians in Illinois and Delaware. More than half said they have treated kids for pain and muscle fatigue caused by backpacks. The Consumer Product Safety Commission found that in 1998 U.S. kids ages 5 to 14 made 10,062 visits to doctor's offices with backpack-caused aches.

Half of the doctors in the A.A.O.S. survey said a backpack can do some damage if it weighs 20 pounds or more. A study by Dr. Charlotte Alexander of Houston, Texas, showed that, on average, kids carry a backpack that weighs 10% of what they weigh. "That's not a problem," says Dr. Alexander, "but we found one 10-year-old with a backpack weighing 47 pounds!"

How should you carry a heavy load? Use both shoulder straps, place the heaviest items closest to your back, and bend both knees when lifting. If you have a lot to carry, try a backpack with hip straps or wheels.

Jordan Morgan is packing lighter now and feeling better. Says Jordan: "I don't fall anymore or hurt myself."

Does your backpack weigh too much?

1. Weigh your backpack.

2. Weigh yourself.

3. Divide your weight by 5.

If your backpack weighs more than this, you could hurt yourself!

A Handy List of Transitional Phrases

Transitional phrases allow the reader to link ideas together. They can be used in the following ways.

To trigger addition:

additionally
also
besides
equally important
furthermore
in addition
moreover
too

To trigger an example:

for example
for instance
thus
in other words
as an illustration
in particular

To trigger emphasis:

above all
after all
again
certainly
indeed
in essence
in fact
in other words
of course
that is to say
to repeat
surely
truly

To trigger a sequence:

afterward
at last
at length
eventually
finally
first
immediately
in the meantime
in time

last
meanwhile
next
previously
respectively
second
secondly
soon
subsequently
then
third
thirdly
today
tomorrow
yesterday

To trigger a summary:

accordingly
after all
as a result
consequently
in any case
in brief
in conclusion
in short
in summary
in the long run
on the whole
to sum up

To trigger granting a point:

at any rate
be that as it may
even so
however
in any case
in any event
in spite of this
nonetheless
still
the fact notwithstanding
while it may be true

To trigger a relationship:

accordingly
alternatively
although
as a result
at the same time
because
but
consequently
conversely
due to
even so
hence
however
in contrast
in the same way
likewise
nevertheless
nonetheless
notwithstanding
on the contrary
on the other hand
similarly
since
still
therefore
thus
while
while this may be true
yet

To trigger a generalization:

all in all
as a rule
as usual
for the most part
generally speaking
in general
on the whole
ordinarily
typically
usually

Adding Transitions

Insert the appropriate words of transition in each blank. In some cases, no word is needed. Try to vary the transitional phrases you select.

1. Some students have ugly pets. _____, Johnny Neimeyer has three hissing beetles, a naked mole rat, and two scorpions. _____, he is trying to convince his parents to buy him a tarantula!

2. Dogs have very sensitive hearing. _____ dogs can hear the sound of a certain whistle, humans cannot.

3. Food manufacturers use peanuts as a filler in many of their products. _____, many children today have developed allergies to peanuts. _____ some experts believe that the consumption of large quantities of processed foods can trigger the allergy.

4. When making pasta, _____ you must boil water. _____ you must add the pasta to the water. _____ you should add the pasta to a sauce.

5. Some entertainers earn millions of dollars a year. _____ public servants barely earn enough money to support their families.

6. Soda pop can irritate the stomach, damage teeth, and trigger a radical drop in sugar levels in the blood stream. _____, drinking large quantities of soda pop is bad for one's health.

7. I used to go to dance lessons every Thursday. _____, I did not enjoy them because I preferred to play my saxophone.

8. Teenagers are misunderstood in our society. _____ many people believe that they are loafers who are causing a lot of crime, _____ teenagers are interesting and productive members of society.

9. _____ that the Russians won the gold medal for pairs skating in the 2002 Olympics, many people believe the Canadians earned it.

10. Jack is quite a character. _____, he is a comedian.

Student Writing Sample

Pamela McLaughlin

Usually people do biographies on people they really know. For example, they do biographies on their friends. My biography is in a way like that, but it's on my role model, my mom.

My mom's name is Pamela Louise McLaughlin. She was born on August 27, 1963 in Denver, Colorado, where she lived for 33 years. She lived in a family of five, with her mom, her step-dad, her two sisters, and herself. Mostly, she spent time with her grandpa who was like a dad to her. She loved her grandpa.

My mom had a lot of adventures when she was a kid. She would ride her bike places, walk places, and do stuff with her friends, like a normal kid except for she wasn't afraid to try something new. For example, if there was some kind of ball hit into a really mean person's backyard, she would go get it. Besides, to her it would be an adventure.

My mom had a hard life as a kid. Her mom was always at work, so she and her sisters would have to make dinner! Every night, my mom would get a call from her mom with directions on how to make dinner. She would tell her sister and they'd all help. Sometimes my mom never had free time because she had sporting events to go to. For example, she loved basketball and field hockey. She played them both and was really good. Eventually, she had to choose one. She chose basketball. She was on a lot of teams as a kid. She played on her school team and was a starter until one day when she got mad at a bad call and slammed the ball down. She got suspended for that year. As a result, now she extremely regrets what she did.

Now my mom is just a mom. She always does stuff with us, though. She is a very talented and nice mom. I'm really glad that she's my mom.

—Joe M.

Style

Objective

The student will write in a way that directly addresses the reader and is unique, compelling, and thoughtful.

Skills

—writing honest, engaging, and personal pieces

—taking risks to reveal the personality of the writer

—interacting with the reader so that he or she can sense who the writer is

Materials

—student copies of "Gramorama!" (page 46)

—writing paper

—student writing sample on page 47 (for teacher reference)

Procedure

1. Begin the lesson with a discussion of style in writing. Explain that style is unique to each writer and that much of the time in school the curriculum is designed to have all students writing in a uniform style. For some assignments, students need to be reminded that they must find their own voice and style.

2. Ask them to close their eyes and imagine that they have woken up in the middle of the night due to an intriguing dream. Ask them to imagine themselves in their usual sleep attire, with hair tossled and eyes bleary. Tell them that they are sitting at the kitchen table across from the only person they feel comfortable being with in this particular state. This is the person to whom they should address their writing.

3. Distribute copies of "Gramorama!" to the students and have them read the article silently.

4. Ask the students to point out places in which the author demonstrates his or her style. Then ask the students how the author is able to demonstrate his or her style. For example, the author uses the word *Gramorama* for his or her grandmother. This conveys his or her personality as well as the grandmother's. The writer is playful and fun and he or she greatly admires the grandma, as demonstrated in the special name. Explain to students that style is created by clever word choice, feeling, and attitude.

Style *(cont.)*

Publication

1. Invite students to write about the best time they ever had. Remind them to include all of the people who were present and to describe their experiences in detail.

2. Ask each student to write about an unusual thing that has happened to him or her or any members of the family. Encourage the student to take risks in his or her writing by exposing real feelings.

3. Ask students to describe a typical holiday celebration with their families. They should write about the experiences in such a way that the reader believes that he or she was present.

Extension

1. Collect a number of stories, columns, and articles that have a distinctive style. Allow students to read and discuss the styles of each and explore how the authors created them.

2. Have students attempt to imitate the style of an author. Be sure to analyze how the author is able to create his or her particular style by answering the following questions:

   What kinds of words does the author use?

   How do these words affect the story?

   How does the author reveal his or her feelings toward the subject?

   What is the author's attitude toward the subject?

   How does the author reveal his or her attitude?

Gramorama!

Most people have a picture in their minds of the perfect grandmother. She's a white-haired, sweet-faced, pleasingly plump homebody. Your basic garden-variety grandma is forever offering freshly baked cookies from her homey kitchen and sage advice from her rocking chair. Right?

Wrong! My Gramorama is five feet, two inches of pure energy and adventure. Forget the white hair; Gram decided on red, so red it is. Or rather, more of a flame color, and always stylish and sleek. She tops the scales at 110 pounds, but don't be fooled by her size. Gramorama knows karate, and she isn't afraid to use it. While she may look pint-sized, Gram is as audacious as they come.

Her apartment might as well not have a kitchen, because Gram puts cooking way down on her priority list. I sometimes think wistfully of the "grandmotherly" types who would tempt me with homemade pies, cakes, and cookies. That would be one traditional "grandmother" trait that would come in handy. But Gram doesn't have time to cook. She's too busy traveling, taking classes, and trying new things.

At least once a year, Gram goes on an adventure vacation. She's seen lion prides and elephant herds in South Africa and ridden a camel in the Gobi Desert. She's been deep-sea fishing off of Mexico and boated down the Amazon River, keeping an eye out for piranha. This year, she may take a whitewater raft trip on the Colorado River or a trek on a glacier in Alaska.

And no napping by the fire on winter evenings, either. Gram says you're never too old to learn, and she's proving it by taking up such subjects as political science, film making, and creative writing at the local college. She showed me the first chapter of her novel—I'm sworn to secrecy—and I think it's great! It's a murder set in . . . hey, wait a minute! I can't tell you. But, of course, the detective is an older woman who looks much younger and has flame-red hair!

Do I wish my grandmother made me chicken soup when I was sick? Told me entertaining stories of what life was like "long ago"? Cheered for every concert, sporting event, and school play? No way! It's much more fun watching a grandmother who has a life and knows how to enjoy it. Instead of holding out for cookies and milk, I'm hoping for a companion ticket on that plane to Alaska with the one and only Gramorama!

Student Writing Sample

Favorite Person

Who is your favorite person? Many people have people who they like or dislike. I, Tammy, have a favorite person. This esteemed person of mine is a very little boy. He is my baby brother.

It was like a normal, sunny day. I went to school, did my homework, ate dinner, and went to bed. I had a very queasy dream. In my dream, I dreamed that my mom was pregnant! The next day, after school, my mom, my sister, and I sat peacefully on the living room couch. Suddenly, my mom said, "I'm pregnant." Thoughts ran through my head. I was going to have a brother that is 10 years apart from me! As days and months passed, my mom's tummy got bigger and bigger. When she put on her seat belt, her tummy would pop out. My grandma, the mother of my mom, came to help us out. She helped and helped. Soon, the day would come. Due to the occasion, my mom and dad had gone to the hospital for the big day. Lois and I were left with my grandma.

It was 12:00 a.m. in the hospital. The doctor had told my mom to walk for two straight hours. So, my mom walked for two straight hours. After that, she waited for the doctor. At 4:00 a.m., my baby brother was born. The next day, I went to visit him. Right when I saw him, I was thinking, "How red!" He was tightly wrapped in cloth so it would be like he was still inside my mom. After one day, my mom and Brandon came home. At last, I had a baby brother!

My brother, Brandon Hyun Ho C., has things he craves for. These things that he craves for are called, "favorites." Brandon's favorite color is green. He thinks it is a boyish color. Equally important, shortbread cookies are his treasured food. "It goes well with a nice, cool drink of Gerber juice," he may think. As the CD player rolls, Brandon enjoys the music of the rap singers.

Nowadays, he is a capricious, mature boy. As an illustration, Brandon's head is 97% bigger, height is 95% taller, and his weight is 90% heavier than a prevalent individual. He has a skin disease, but not too bad, so he cannot eat much meat, cow's milk, and other bad foods. Sometimes, he is a very bad boy. Even so, he is still my most cherished person.

In the long run, this is my favorite person. He is a smart little boy and will always be my most adored boy.

—Tammy C.

Feeling

Objective

The student will develop a style in writing that is unique and engaging and with feeling in order to add interest and evoke emotion in the reader.

Skills

—identify how feeling and emotion add interest to the message of a piece of writing

—using feeling and emotion to add interest to the message of a piece of writing

—interacting with the reader to help create a sense of the writer's personality

—writing pieces that are honest, personal, and engaging

Materials

—advertisements from magazines

—student copies of "A Note for Rachel Scott" (page 50)

—writing paper

—student writing sample on page 51 (for teacher reference)

Procedure

1. Provide students with a variety of magazine advertisements to examine. Be sure to select many ads that appeal to emotions (vanity, fear, etc.) and to a sense of duty.

2. Have each student choose one ad to write about and ask him or her to explain how the ad appeals to emotions.

3. Invite students to show and explain their ads to the class.

4. Ask the students which advertisements they believe are the most effective. Lead the class in a discussion about how the advertisers are able to evoke emotional responses in consumers through ads. In essence, advertisers are able to compel the consumers to buy their products by causing them to have emotional responses. Usually, these emotions are commonly felt among most of us. For example, most people feel patriotic. Therefore, ads that contain red, white, and blue appeal to our sense of duty to our country.

5. Explain how appealing to emotions in advertising is similar to appealing to emotions in writing. Sometimes the goal of writing is to make the reader feel something, and that can only be accomplished through the words the writer chooses. Students must decide which words to use and how to put them together in order to appeal to their readers' feelings.

6. Distribute copies of "A Note for Rachel Scott" to the students.

Feeling *(cont.)*

7. Ask students to look for places in the letter in which the author causes them to feel an emotion. Ask the students to look for how the author expresses his or her feelings. The author writes about Rachel's friends writing goodbye messages to her. Just mentioning a white casket creates an image of a funeral and the feeling of loss. The author also writes that Rachel was a young writer and the readers of the article can most likely identify with this. Moreover, the structure of the article is very powerful. As an open letter, the author is able to be much more direct, intimate, and candid about feelings about what happened to Rachel because it is more personal than an editorial or a factual article. When we read how one person reacts emotionally to an experience, it helps us to think about our own feelings about the experience.

8. Ask the students to look for ways the author seems to reveal himself or herself to the reader. Does the author take a risk to reveal his vulnerabilities?

9. Have the students write open letters in a similar manner to anyone—dead or alive. Encourage them to work to appeal to the readers' feelings and to personalize their work.

Publication

1. Have each student take the letter home to share with a family member. The family member should write a response to the letter in which he or she explains if and how the work stirred an emotional response.

2. Have students bring in pictures to accompany their open letters. Using the pictures and letters, make a class book.

Extension

1. Invite students to write about a recent news event about which they had strong feelings. Have selected students write in different forms—journal entries, factual articles, editorials, etc. Compare and contrast the different styles and their abilities to express the emotion of the writer.

2. Have each student choose an emotion—happiness, sadness, anger, boredom, bravery, fear—and try to illustrate that feeling in sentences using sensory details. For example, excitement might be seen as a cork popping off of a bottle with the carbonation bubbling out, heard as a child clapping and yelling, felt like the tingling sensation on skin, smelled as the air on a fresh, autumn day, or tasted as sweet candy popping and crackling in the mouth.

3. Have students collect examples of newspaper and magazine articles that evoke emotional responses. Ask them to highlight where the author makes them feel an emotion.

A Note for Rachel Scott

Your friends were shown on television, writing goodbye messages on the white casket provided for you. I hope you will not mind if a stranger writes a message of his own. Of course, this is a literary device (as a young writer, you will recognize it as such), a way of doing an essay on the thoughts your death evokes. But this is also for you alone, Rachel, dead at 17, yet ineradicable because of the photograph of your bright and witty face, now sadly familiar to the country, and because of the loving and admiring testimonies of your family.

Your dad said in an interview last week that while there were many legal and legislative questions to be answered in the aftermath of the Columbine High School murders, these did not touch "the deep issues of the heart." He was referring specifically to the forgiveness that he, your mother and stepfather were dredging up for your killers, Dylan and Eric.

But the issue I want to touch upon has to do with me and colleagues—journalists who, for all our recurrent, unusually unattractive displays of know-it-all confidence, occasionally come upon a story such as yours and recognize our helplessness before it.

So, Rachel, when I write, "This is what I want to tell you," please read, "This is what I want to ask": Where do we, who ply our trade in magazines and elsewhere, find the knowledge of the unknowable? How do we learn to trust the unknowable as news—those deep issues of the heart?

Journalists are pretty good at unearthing the undeep issues. Give us a presidential scandal, even a war, and we can do a fair job of explaining the explicable. But give us the killings at Columbine, and in an effort to cover the possibilities we will miss what people are thinking and feeling in their secret chambers—about their own loves and hatreds, about the necessity of attentiveness to others, about their own children: about you, Rachel.

The only question that ever ought to matter to my colleagues and our customers is the one we do not ask except in retrospect, after the guns or the scandal: Who are we all in silence—at a table in the cafeteria, at a table in the library? What can journalists tell others about the mind we all share, the innocent mind and the murderous? That is the real news of your death.

I would like to have remembered it before Tuesday, April 20, 1999, when the news of the day supposedly brought you to light. Rachel, you were always in the light. And that's the one thing none of us can forget.

Student Writing Sample

Letter to Danielle

Dear Danielle Van Damme,

   Your parents are very worried about you and wish that you would come home soon. Everyone has been looking for you. I see your picture on pieces of paper in every store I go to, and it makes me sad and scared. Did you run away? Did someone take you from your room in the middle of the night? I can't sleep since you disappeared because I'm scared someone is going to take me. My mom lets me sleep with her, but don't tell anyone because I am embarrassed. You seem like a nice girl and when you get home, maybe we can ride bikes together. Come home soon because we are worried.

                                     Love,
                                     Serena

                              —*Serena T.*

Tone

Objective

The student will understand and utilize word choice, details, imagery, and language to convey attitude toward the subject in their writing.

Skills

—understanding an author's attitude in a piece of writing

—identifying and interpreting multiple tones in one piece of writing

—utilizing word choice, details, imagery, and diction to create tone in writing

Materials

—student copies of "The Bus Ride" (page 54)

—student copies of "Tone Activity" (page 55)

—chalkboard

—writing paper

—student writing sample on page 56 (for teacher reference)

Procedure

1. Begin by distributing copies of "The Bus Ride" to students. Read the article aloud to the class as they follow along. Ask the students to identify the author's attitude toward the bus ride as you read.

2. Point out that the author's attitude toward the bus ride shifts during the story. How do they know what the author's attitude is? Ask the students to support their choices with examples from the story.

3. Discuss in great detail the author's word choice, details, imagery, and the types of words chosen in the article.

4. To introduce the topic of tone, speak the same phrase using several different tones of voice. The phrases "Come here" or "Not now" might be said threateningly, passively, sweetly, pleadingly, mysteriously, etc.

5. Explain that when we hear people talking, we can tell the tone of their words by the inflection in their voices. However, in writing, we only have the words, so we must use details, imagery and diction in order to make the tone of our writing clear to the reader.

6. Distribute copies of "Tone Activity" to the students to complete.

7. Divide the students into groups of two and select several groups to present the dialogue using different tones in front of the class. Encourage them to use gestures, sounds, and expression to add to the tone.

Tone *(cont.)*

8. After the presentations, ask the students how they could change the words of the dialogue to make the scene clearer to the reader. Have the pairs of students who did not do the dialogue in front of the class explain their ideas to the rest of the class.

9. Have a student write the suggestions on the chalkboard for the class to see. (Encourage them to use verbs that suggest tone, such as mutter, sigh, yell.)

Publication

1. Ask students to rewrite the dialogue created in the lesson on tone into a paragraph in which they use precise word choice, details, imagery, and language to demonstrate the tone.

2. Ask each student to write about a time when he or she had a change of heart about something. Encourage the student to use precise word choice, details, imagery, and language to create two distinct tones (before and after their change of heart) about the experience.

3. Have students trade papers with classmates to determine if the tone of the writing is clear.

Extension

1. On each of several index cards, write the names of different attitudes or tones. Distribute them to the class. Ask the students to make up short, simple dialogue exemplifying the tone on the card.

2. Ask students to bring in examples of a variety of tones. Place the examples on a bulletin board in the classroom.

The Bus Ride

The winter wind ripped across Minneapolis and tore through the skyscrapers. It finally smacked against me so hard that my feet literally left the icy pavement. As I brushed an icicle from the tip of my nose, I thought, this is it. It's too cold. The bus is never going to arrive, and my graduate school classmates will find me lying here. Because no one, I decided, can survive winter in Minneapolis.

Then the bus pulled up. It seemed that all the people who live in the Minneapolis metropolitan area had the exact same idea to ride this exact bus at this exact time. As I shoved against the wall of people, I wished for a giant shoehorn. Somehow, I wedged myself onboard, and the collective body of the bus absorbed me. I stood holding the handrail as the bus started to move.

Something jabbed me in the back. I ignored it. Or tried to ignore it. The suffocating effects of city life were reaching an intolerable level. I was jabbed in the back again. And—strike three!—again. That was it. I couldn't take anymore. All the pushing, the shoving, the jabbing!

I whirled around. Turning so violently in the tightly packed conditions produced the same effect as pulling out the bottom layer from a stack of blocks. Everything tumbled and shifted as passengers around me struggled to find their balance. Too bad, I thought. I was having a bad day and now they would too.

I discovered the source of the jabbing. It was the corner of a white cake box. Currently, the cake box was being juggled back and forth in the mittened hands of a young woman. She was about twenty-three and wore a bright red hat. On her coat was a button that read: Have a great day!

My first reaction was not a kind one. I hesitated to help her and, in that moment, the box went crashing to the wet floor.

The woman squealed and reached for the box. There wasn't enough room for her to bend and pick it up. But I was already moving. I sank straight down like a diver going into the murky depths of a dangerous ocean and plucked up the box by its blue ribbon.

"Thank you," she said, taking it from me.

"I'm sorry," I said. And I was. I had been a jerk and now look what I had done. One side of the box had been opened, and I could see the smashed cake that was inside.

"It's okay," she said. "You couldn't know this was my first day in Minneapolis." She took a breath. "And my birthday."

My heart skipped a beat. I imagined her all alone in her new, empty apartment with nothing but birthday candles to keep her warm. And now I had ruined even that for her. "I am sorry," I repeated.

She just smiled and said, "Well, all cake tastes the same. Squished or not."

I'd like to say I burst into song and led the whole bus in a rousing rendition of "Happy Birthday." Or that I gave her a winning lottery ticket. Or presented her with a new car.

No. I can't say any of that happened.

But I did give her the rest of my life. Because, you see, on that cold, miserable winter morning on a bus in Minneapolis was where and when I met my wife.

And it was her birthday.

Tone Activity

Read the following dialogue with your partner.

A:	What is this?
B:	It's for you.
A:	It is?
B:	Yes.
A:	It's too late.
B:	I know. I couldn't help it.
A:	I understand.

Think about the way this scene could be played in the following ways:

- by a teacher and student who has late work

- a pair of siblings who are angry at each other

- a couple who might split up

- spies in need of equipment for surveillance

In each scenario the tone controls the audience's understanding and interpretation. Your emphasis and inflection as you pronounce the words will determine the meaning for your listeners.

Student Writing Sample

The Teacher and the Student

When Kelly came to school on Monday, she handed a paper to her teacher. Mrs. M. stared down her nose at her with a look of anger. "What's this?" she asked with irritation in her voice.

Kelly responded timidly, "It's for you." Mrs. M. barely heard her. Kelly's voice was so quiet, almost like a mouse.

"It is?" Mrs. M. asked, surprised.

"Yes," whispered Kelly, ashamed.

Mrs. M. looked at her calendar. The paper was two weeks and one day late. This was way passed the extra time Mrs. M. gave to students. She looked at Kelly with a sad look on her face and said, "It's too late."

Kelly looked crushed. "I know. I couldn't help it," she said apologetically.

"I understand," said Mrs. M. forgivingly. She had a look on her face that seemed to say that everything was going to be okay.

Kelly felt better.

—June I.

Narrative Voice

Objective

The student will capture and hold the reader's attention by creating the illusion of reality when using the narrative voice.

Skills

—capturing and holding the reader's attention by using the elements of subject matter, suspense, climax, and time in narrative writing

—creating the illusion of reality with word choice, diction, dialogue, setting, character development, and details

Materials

—sheets of paper
—student copies of "Toss Me a Line!" (page 59)
—student copies of "Narrative Voice" (page 60)
—writing paper
—student writing sample on page 61 (for teacher reference)

Procedure

1. Ask the class to think back to their earliest memories of school. What incident stands out the most? Why?

2. Ask them to visualize the experience and review all of the details they need in order to be able to tell the experience to another person.

3. Ask for a student volunteer to share his or her story with the class. As the class listens, have each student write down the elements of the story that contribute to creating the narrative voice. These are subject matter, suspense, climax, and time.

4. Ask the students to pay attention to word choice, diction, dialogue, setting, character development, and details that stand out. Feel free to lead students who seem to have stage fright.

5. Review the student volunteer's story and elements of narrative in the story. If time permits, allow another student to share his or her story, and have the rest of the class track the narrative devices.

6. As students continue to tell their stories, encourage each consecutive student to improve upon the narrative skills of the previous story.

7. Distribute student copies of "Toss Me a Line!" and "Narrative Voice." Have the students take turns reading portions of the story aloud and then complete the activity page.

8. Review the answers on the activity page.

Narrative Voice *(cont.)*

9. Have students think about proverbs, such as:

    - The early bird gets the worm.
    - He who hesitates is lost.
    - All's well that ends well.
    - All that glitters is not gold.
    - A friend in need is a friend indeed.
    - Nothing ventured, nothing gained.
    - Birds of a feather flock together.
    - Don't put off till tomorrow what you can do today.
    - Necessity is the mother of invention.
    - Do unto others as you would have them do unto you.

10. Have each student choose a personal experience for which a proverb would make an appropriate title.

11. Then have each student narrate the experience briefly in such a way that their readers will see their point with little or no direct explanation from them.

Publication

1. Have the students make their stories into children's books with illustrations for the younger students at your school. Donate the books to these classes or allow them to borrow the books for a period of time. Allow your students to read their tales to the younger children.

2. Have the students create a class newspaper in which they include the stories.

Extension

1. Provide the class with many examples of narratives. Ask students to identify the different elements of a narrative.

2. Have students choose any fairly short television drama or comedy that they enjoyed and that made a strong point. Have them retell the program as a story, with full background detail.

Toss Me a Line!

It's one of those horrors you hear people talk about. You're on stage in the middle of a play. The actors, the audience—everyone—is waiting for you to speak. But you can't remember your lines. Unfortunately for me, this was not a nightmare. This was real. I stood frozen on the long stairway of the set for the musical *Mame*.

How did I—a clumsy linebacker on the school football team—get here? It's simple: That afternoon, Mrs. Smela, our high school drama teacher, had sprinted up to me in the hall, her crazy hair standing straight up like cobras reacting to a snake charmer's music. "One of my actors is out sick!" she shouted at me. "He has just one line and you're the only one who fits his costume! Please, Stan, please, say you'll do it!"

I felt sorry for her and said, "Sure." I mumbled something about how the show must go on.

"You won't regret your decision!" she bellowed, patting me on the arm. But now, in the middle of the performance, I think no one regretted my decision more than she did. On stage, I opened my mouth to speak. Nothing came out.

My mind raced. I knew the scene called for a toast. All the actors had raised their glasses full of grape juice, and now I was supposed to say something. What that something was, I couldn't tell you if my life depended on it. Not only had I forgotten my line, but I also couldn't breathe, swallow, even blink.

And that's not good if you wear contact lenses.

Doink! With an audible sound, the contact lens popped out of my left eye and whizzed toward the audience. I didn't think, "Hey, I'm on stage in a play. There are 450 parents and friends watching me." I thought, "Holy cow! That's my expensive contact lens!"

In one motion, I tossed aside my glass of grape juice—barely noticing the purple juice splatter the guy next to me—and plucked the flying lens out of the tension-filled air.

In the process, my arm accidentally pushed against Andrea Marozas, the girl playing Mame. She lost her balance and stumbled down the stairway. Sure, she lost her step and banged down the steps like a cement Slinky. But she was good. By the end of the stumble, she managed to turn her movements into a little disco-like dance. (I hear she's working in a big New York City theater now. Of course, I hear about this through other people. Andrea's still not talking to me after that night.)

At that moment, I wasn't interested in evaluating her performance. I was too busy wondering, "How can I keep my contact lens moist so it doesn't crumble?"

Without thinking, I stepped down to Andrea. I snatched the glass out of her hand and plopped the contact lens in it. She gave me a look that would have driven Sir Laurence Olivier from the stage, screaming in terror.

"Darling," she hissed at me, a fake smile plastered on her face. "You're such a silly! I want to give a toast!" She grabbed her glass back. "To life!" she screamed quickly, worried I'd interrupt again.

And then she drank the juice from the cup. All of it, including my contact lens.

No one was happier—with the exceptions of Andrea and Mrs. Smela—than I when I returned to the football field. In football, the only lines I had to remember were "Grrr!" and "Get out of my way!"

Narrative Voice

When reading, "Toss Me A Line!" pay close attention to the elements of a narrative. In complete sentences, answer the following questions.

1. What is the subject matter of the story?
   _____

2. Why is the subject matter funny?
   _____
   _____

3. When is the story suspenseful?
   _____
   _____

4. How does the writer create suspense?
   _____
   _____

5. What is the climax of the story?
   _____
   _____

6. How does the writer of the story handle time? Is it sequenced? Does the author compress or expand time?
   _____
   _____
   _____

7. What specific words does the author use that help make the story seem more real?
   _____

8. What concrete and specific diction does the author use to help you hear, taste, smell, and feel the events in the story?
   _____
   _____

9. Do you get a better sense of the action, suspense, the characters, the setting, etc., through the dialogue? Explain.
   _____

10. What is the setting? How is it described?
    _____

11. Describe the characters in the story? What do you think of them? Why?
    _____
    _____

12. What specific details help you to better understand any element of the story?
    _____
    _____

Student Writing Sample

On Being Helpful

My mom is always telling us to clean up, but my brother and I don't like to clean up. Sometimes I clean up when I make a mess, but not my brother. He never cleans anything.

One day my mom told us to clean up all our sports stuff in the garage, but my brother wouldn't stop reading *Harry Potter* to do it, so I cleaned it up by myself. I was really mad when I was putting the junk away. I always work and my brother never works. Why doesn't he have to clean?

The next day when my brother went outside to play basketball, my mom went out to talk to him. She told him he couldn't play basketball because he didn't put the sports stuff away like she asked. He couldn't use his basketball for a week, she said. And then she took me to the store to buy a new soccer ball. She said I earned it. But my brother didn't get one and he wouldn't be allowed to use mine.

Ever since then my brother has been more helpful.

—*Alyssa T.*

Descriptive Voice

Objectives

The student will establish and develop a plot and setting.

The student will present a point of view that is appropriate to the story, include sensory details, and concrete language to develop plot and character.

The student will use a range of narrative devices.

Skills

—narrate an event

—recognizing and utilizing sensory details

—identifying and using the element of suspense or surprise

—utilizing interior dialogue and dialogue among characters

—incorporating visual details

— using feelings and insights to enrich story telling

Materials

—student copies of "Panic in Paris" (page 64)

—index cards

—markers

—student copies of "15 Seconds of Fame" (pages 65–67)

—writing paper

—student writing sample on page 68 (for teacher reference)

Procedure

1. Distribute student copies of "Panic in Paris."

2. Have students take turns reading portions of the narrative aloud to the class. When students have finished reading, review the elements of a narrative with them.

3. Prepare a set of index cards with one of the following terms on each—*narrative action, suspense or surprise, interior monologue, specific names, dialogue, visual details, sensory description, feelings,* and *insights*.

4. Divide the students into nine groups and distribute one index card to each of the groups.

5. Have the students work together to find examples of the various narrative devices in "Panic in Paris." Ask one student from the group to present the groups' findings to the rest of the class.

6. Discuss narrative techniques in general with the students. Use examples from well-known stories and ask the students to provide examples of the techniques from those stories.

Descriptive Voice *(cont.)*

7. Distribute copies of pages 65–67, "15 Seconds of Fame" to the students. Ask them to complete the pages in preparation for writing an autobiographical incident essay.

8. Instruct each student to write an autobiographical essay.

Publication

1. Allow students to share their stories with each other in read-around groups.

2. Have the students nominate which essays should be read aloud to the entire class.

3. Create a class book of the essays. Display the book prominently in the class for all to read.

Extension

1. Allow time in class for students to peruse the Internet for additional information on narrative techniques and voice. Require each student to find one item of interest for the class to view. (Be sure to monitor all Internet use in order to ensure student safety.)

2. If desired, prepare an Internet treasure hunt for students in which they read narratives online. Require them to identify the narrative techniques in at least one of the pages you have them view.

Panic in Paris

The elevator door slid open. The crowd inside let out a collective gasp of excitement. But no one was more excited than my mom. This 110-pound woman is not normally rude, but suddenly she had all the courtesy of a linebacker diving for a fumble. My mom charged through the door, nearly knocking over an elderly, German tourist.

Great, I thought, just what we need: an international incident.

My mom wasn't interested in the sights, she just wanted air. If there's one thing that frightens my mom more than cramped spaces, it's heights. And we were now 889 feet above the Paris cityscape. Maybe we should have taken the Eiffel Tower off our "to do" list.

By the time I caught up with her, she had pressed her entire body against a huge steel girder that zig-zagged through the structure. The Eiffel Tower was her giant teddy bear. I couldn't help but laugh.

"What?" she said defensively, her arms wrapping around the support and her face flushed. "I'm having a great time."

"Yeah, I can tell. Let's go," I said.

Amidst the twinkling reflection of the City of Lights, I saw terror in her eyes. She was so scared of heights, she couldn't move. I imagined French experts dropping from helicopters in a desperate attempt to free their beloved Tower from the crushing hug of this tiny American.

I was going to have to think of something—and fast.

"I know, Mom!" I shouted, making her jump. "We don't have to get back in the elevator. We can walk all the way down." Before she could think about it, I took her arm and led her over to the stairs.

Hoping to distract her, I pulled out our Paris guidebook and called out the facts about the Tower as we made our way down. There's a total of 1,652 steps. Forty tons of paint are used on the Tower every year. The Tower sways about 4 inches in strong winds.

Judging from my mom's horrified gasp, this last fact was one I didn't need to share. We kept walking for twenty long minutes.

Finally, we headed down the last flight. I pushed the steel exit gate. "See? That wasn't so bad . . . ."

The gate didn't move. I felt a twinge of panic. I pushed again, still no movement. Were we trapped? My hands repositioned for better leverage. I shoved again against the gate. Out of breath, I felt on the verge of tears. I hated being locked in. What was wrong with this door!

"Qu'est-ce que c'est la probleme?"

A young French security guard stood on the other side of the gate. He repeated his question. The fact that I didn't understand French only made me panic more. I banged violently on the door, rocked against it. Still nothing.

The guard smiled now. He pointed up and said in English, "The sign. Read it."

I followed his pointing finger to a sign that hung above the gate. It said: "Tirez." I looked at the guard blankly. What did that mean?

"The sign," the guard told me. "It says, 'Pull.'"

Stepping back, I stopped pushing the gate. I pulled instead. It swung open easily on greased hinges. Now my face burned from embarrassment, not panic.

"Karen, you really need to learn to relax," my mom said, laughing as she breezed past me.

15 Seconds of Fame

The Autobiographical Incident

Pick a memory from your life to share with others. The memory could be a minute long, a few hours, or a couple of days. Your life is important and must be remembered so that when you are 80 years old, your memories of times past will keep you feeling alive.

Think of a memorable moment in your life:

_____

_____

For five minutes, write about this moment:

_____

_____

_____

_____

_____

_____

_____

_____

_____

_____

(Narrative Action) Tell about what happened in this moment:

_____

_____

_____

_____

_____

15 Seconds of Fame *(cont.)*

(*Suspense/Surprise*) What could be mysterious or surprising about the moment in your life?

_____

_____

_____

_____

(*Interior Monologue*) Tell what was going through your mind as this moment happened:

_____

_____

_____

_____

(*Specific Names*) Who was involved with the incident?

_____

_____

_____

_____

(*Dialogue*) What do you remember saying or talking about during the incident? Write down, word for word, what was said: _____

_____

_____

_____

(*Visual Details*) Write down the objects, colors, shapes, and movements you remember seeing during this moment: _____

_____

_____

_____

15 Seconds of Fame *(cont.)*

(*Sensory Description*) Write down what you heard, touched, smelled, and tasted during this moment: _____

_____

_____

_____

_____

_____

(*Feelings*) Write down all the feelings you had during this moment:

_____

_____

_____

_____

_____

Draw a picture from this moment in your life:

Student Writing Sample

Autobiographical Essay

I think that the best time I ever had was when my soccer team (Encinitas Express) beat the best team in the league (Temecula). They had beaten us about five times, so we considered them our arch enemies and today we were going to play them on their home turf. They had beaten us many times on our home turf, so they were expecting to win. We watched them already celebrating their "win." We had to have lunch together win or lose, and they thought we would lose just because we were so far away from home.

In the first five minutes of the game Temecula scores, and in the next ten minutes they almost score another goal, but we save it. Finally it is halftime, and they are ahead 1–0. Our coach begins her halftime speech and says, "Every pro player takes about 15 shots to every goal. Wouldn't you agree?" We all agreed. "Well, I want you to go out there and beat those pros record!" And we did.

After about five shots, Hannah Katkov got the ball and scored from the midfield line. About 10 minutes later, we were at 10 shots and Maddie Lyon on defense got the ball and kicked it up the field to Audre, and Audre passed to me. I shot, and I scored! The coach took me off the field with five minutes left . . . four. . . . three . . . I'm back on the field. Two minutes later, the final whistle blew. We won the game! Lunch became our time to celebrate our win.

—Alex M.

Expository Voice

Objective

The student will write an informational essay that includes adequate examples to support a topic.

Skills

—understanding the difference between expository, narrative, and descriptive writing
—brainstorming a variety of topics
—providing adequate examples to support a topic
—writing an informational essay

Materials

—student copies of "The Last Orangutans" (page 71)
—writing paper
—student writing sample on page 72 (for teacher reference)

Procedure

1. Begin by helping the students to understand the distinction between expository writing and writing that is primarily narrative or descriptive. While expository writing often contains description, its purpose is different.

2. Explain that the purpose of expository writing is to inform, explain, analyze or interpret, and as a result, it is probably the most common form of writing required in schools. We are often asked to explain why we are late getting home from the movies, what caused the Civil War, or how to get to the zoo. The structures of expository writing often include process writing (the how-to essay), cause and effect, problem and solution, question and answer, and comparison and contrast.

3. Distribute copies of "The Last Orangutans" to the students. Ask them to identify the author's main idea and the facts that are used to support it.

4. Ask the students to identify the places where the author uses description to inform the readers. Be sure to remind them that, although the article does include description, the voice is distinct because the structure, content, and function of the article are different than in narrative writing.

5. Encourage students to identify the author's audience for the article. The author seems to assume that the reader knows very little about the topic. This helps to inform all potential readers and makes the writing more convincing.

6. Ask students to brainstorm a list of expository topics as you record them on the chalkboard.

7. If a topic that is more narrative or descriptive in nature is selected, such as *my bedroom* or *my family*, ask the students how the topic could be treated in an expository essay. What would they explain? What facts or information would they present? The essay might, for example, focus on how kids today need more personal space than in the past and they would use their own bedroom needs as examples to illustrate the point.

Expository Voice *(cont.)*

8. Ask students to choose public figures they particularly admire, such as a television or movie actor, a musician, or an athlete, and write expository essays explaining the reasons for their admiration. Each student should assume that the readers know little about the person, and he or she should support claims with several examples.

Publication

1. Send copies of the revised and edited essays to their subjects. If students receive responses, they will be thrilled.

2. Hold a read-aloud session of the essays in class and ask students to vote on which student's essay is the most convincing.

Extension

1. Have students choose one of the appropriate topics brainstormed in class for expository writing. Allow students adequate time to research their topics for facts, statistics, and examples.

2. Have students write how-to essays in which they teach a reader a new skill. Make sure they include at the beginning of their essays the lists of materials needed. Have them assume their readers are completely unfamiliar with the topics.

The Last Orangutans

According to the Dayak people of Borneo, orangutans can talk; they simply hide the fact to avoid being put to work. The theory is not entirely implausible. Humans and orangutans are 97 percent identical in terms of DNA. Only chimpanzees, with nearly 99 percent, and gorillas with 98 percent, are more closely related to us.

Once common across Southeast Asia, orangutans are now found only on the islands of Borneo (divided among Indonesia, Malaysia, and Brunei) and Sumatra (part of Indonesia). Over the past two decades, thanks to a boom in logging and plantation agriculture, the rain forests where they live have shrunk by 80 percent. Since 1987 the wild orangutan population has plummeted from an estimated 180,000 to 27,000.

Fortunately, the orangutans have a determined ally. Birkute Galdikas, a German-born Canadian with an Indonesian passport, was inspired by paleontologist Louis Leakey to spend her life among nonhuman primates. For 27 years she has studied orangutans at Camp Leakey, her compound in Indonesian Borneo, braving leopards, bears, cobras, pythons, leeches, and tropical diseases. She has rescued and rehabilitated scores of displaced orangutans and traveled the world to plead their case. In the process, she has provided her staff—all Dayak, as is her husband and codirector, Pak Bohap—with a way to earn a living while protecting their environment.

As their habitat dwindles, orangutans increasingly cross paths with humans. The adults, notorious garden raiders, are often killed and sometimes eaten. But their cuddly orphans are a hot commodity. Poachers sell them as exotic pets. When they get too big and unruly to handle—adult males can weigh 250 pounds—many are imprisoned in cages or sold to traders who supply zoos.

Luckier captives, surrendered by their owners or confiscated by government authorities, land in one of five rehab centers scattered throughout orangutan country. Camp Leakey is among the oldest, providing food, medical care, and survival training until its guests are ready to set up housekeeping in relatively safe areas of the jungle. Galdikas and her assistants act as foster parents for as long as eight years, the time an orangutan mother would normally spend raising her child. Infants get plenty of snuggling. Youngsters are taken on field trips into the forest, where they learn by observation and experimentation what fruits, leaves, and grubs are best to eat, and how to make their nightly nests.

Quiet and contemplative, orangutans seldom resort to violence unless they feel threatened—or their sense of dignity is violated. Galdikas tells the story of an American volunteer who tried to herd a reluctant female toward Camp Leakey's feeding station by waving a stick. "She walked over to the man, took the stick away and started hitting him with it. The next thing I knew, she was driving him in front of her!"

Outside Camp Leakey it is harder for orangutans to get the upper hand. But with Galdikas's help, they may have a chance at survival.

Student Writing Sample

Expository Writing

　　Martina Hingis is one of the youngest tennis players in the world. She has won many awards and is in the top ten in women's tennis. I admire her because of her wonderful athletic performance and excellent tennis skills. She is strong and she has good stamina. I think she is very pretty and is a great sport. I feel she's a very special tennis player also because she comes from Switzerland like me. I hope she does well in her next match.

—Elena C.

Persuasive Voice

Objective

The student will develop an argument, sequence ideas, and use techniques to persuade for a persuasive essay.

Skills

—identifying persuasive techniques in writing

—developing an argument for a persuasive essay

—sequencing the evidence in an argument for a dramatic effect

—writing a persuasive essay

Materials

—student copies of "Brand-Name Schools" (page 75)

—student copies of "Presenting a Persuasive Argument" (page 76)

—writing paper

—student writing sample on page 77 (for teacher reference)

Procedure

1. Distribute copies of "Brand-Name Schools" to the students. Read the article as a class. Have students identify the argument and evidence the author uses to convince the reader of his or her opinion.

2. Ask students to evaluate how the author persuades the audience to believe the argument. Ask the students the following questions:

Does the author:

—appeal to the reader's emotions?

—appeal to the reader's interests and sympathies?

—appeal to logic?

—use a dramatic incident to illustrate a point?

—explain the process of how something was, is, or might be?

—give a clear definition of a key term?

—ask any questions and then answer them?

—use dramatic effect by exaggerating or use an analogy?

—present counter-arguments by showing other points of view?

—show the weaknesses and strengths of the opposing points of view?

—end by presenting the strongest argument?

—offer a solution to the problem?

Persuasive Voice *(cont.)*

3. Present a problem to the students about your school or community. Ask the students to decide on a problem they want solved. For example, the bathrooms do not have hot water, the lunches are not tasty, the playground equipment is unstable, the park lacks benches, or the medians are dull and boring.

4. Once the students have decided on an issue, have them work in pairs to develop a statement of the problem that is clear, concise, and powerful.

5. Distribute copies of "Presenting a Persuasive Argument" to the students. Have them begin to answer the questions.

6. Ask students to brainstorm a list of the reasons they will use to persuade the person in charge to correct the problem. Record the list on the chalkboard for the class to view.

7. Have students reorder the list from the board onto the activity page from least to most convincing.

8. Next, inform the students that convincing evidence is not always enough to accomplish goals. There are also techniques writers use to persuade others of their viewpoint. Remind them of the techniques used in "Brand-Name Schools" and require them to use these techniques as they convince their reader to correct the problem they have selected.

9. Have the students work in groups of five and assign each a specific paragraph to write for the essay. Assign one student the task of the introduction, two students the task of writing the body, one student the task of writing the conclusion, and one student the task of selecting an appropriate title and piecing together the essay using effective transitions and repetition to achieve coherence and unity. Encourage students to use the information in the activity page to help them organize and present their ideas.

Publication

1. Send the letters to the local newspaper for publication in the editorial section.

2. If the issue is related to your school, send the letters to the members of the school board and the principal.

Extension

1. Find many examples of persuasive writing and have students identify all of the techniques used to convince the reader to change his or her mind about an issue.

2. Have students write persuasive letters to their parents about issues at home that they want changed. Be sure to advise students to choose appropriate topics (driving at age 11 is not appropriate, but increased allowance or a later bedtime might be).

Brand-Name Schools

Imagine going to a school where the uniforms are made by Nike, the cafeteria food comes from Pizza Hut, and the math lessons involve adding and subtracting M&M's, then eating the answer.

This is a realistic scene is some schools, which have made deals with big companies. Companies are bringing brand-name products and advertisements into schools. They are distracting kids from learning and turning classes into all-day commercials. Public schools should not be making these kinds of deals.

PEPSI-ONLY SCHOOLS

Public schools get most of their money from state and local governments, which collect it from taxpayers. That money pays for books, buildings and teachers' salaries, but schools are often looking for extra funds.

More and more of them are turning to companies that sell products to kids. These companies, such as Pepsi and Pizza Hut, agree to pay schools for the right to advertise and sell their products in school cafeterias, classrooms, and stadiums. The companies figure that if kids start buying their stuff today, they will continue buying it when they're grown-ups.

Big companies are willing to pay big bucks to promote their brands in schools. In 1998, Pepsi paid $5.75 million to the school system of Denver, Colorado. For the next five years, all Denver public schools will carry only Pepsi-brand drinks in vending machines. The deal also gives Pepsi the right to splash its logo throughout the school. In another Colorado district, Coke paid $5.5 million to be the only soda in school.

WHAT'S THE COST?

Television, magazines, movies—they all aim ads at kids. It's bad enough that kids are bombarded by ads outside of school. Why make kids pay attention to ads in school as well? Such advertising encourages kids to think about spending money rather than doing schoolwork. It is not right to brainwash kids into preferring certain brands. Says Dave DiGiacomo, a school-board member in Jefferson County, Colorado: "Schools shouldn't sell minds to the highest bidder."

However, other school officials, like John Bushey of Colorado Springs, argue that school advertising "doesn't interfere with education." His district signed an $8 million deal with Coke in 1997. The money will help pay for musical instruments, athletic equipment, and other expenses. School districts in California, Florida, and Maryland are also considering joining up with big companies.

Schools need to find other ways to earn extra money. They shouldn't use kids as pawns in their advertising campaigns.

Presenting a Persuasive Argument

The topic for the argument is: _____

A clear and powerful statement of the argument is:_____

The reasons I have for this argument are:

1. _____
2. _____
3. _____
4. _____
5. _____
6. _____
7. _____

I should eliminate the following reasons because they are not strong enough:

_____

_____

_____

If I reorder the reasons from least persuasive to most persuasive they are:

1. _____
2. _____
3. _____
4. _____

I will use the following techniques to develop the body paragraphs:

_____

_____

_____

_____

What are the counter-arguments to my argument? How can I discredit them?

_____

_____

What is the solution to my problem?

_____

_____

Student Writing Sample

A Hot Problem

Our school should have hot water in the bathrooms. When we go to the bathroom and try to use the hot water, nothing comes out. Having no hot water makes us feel unimportant. We go to a nice school, but when it is very cold outside, it is too cold to wash our hands in the sinks. The water is like ice, it is so cold. So some kids don't wash their hands after they go to the bathroom. That's gross. Most importantly, cold water can't kill germs from when we get dirty, so washing our hands is a waste of time.

Have you ever gone to the bathroom to wash your hands and had nothing come out of the faucet? It is a little embarrassing and surprising when it happens. I mean, there is a handle for the hot water, but no hot water comes. It makes people feel unimportant when no water is there. It's like the school is too cheap to use hot water. We are important enough for hot water because we are the students. Without us, there would be no school in the first place.

A few weeks ago it was really cold outside because it was raining and hailing even. I went to the bathroom and when I turned on the water to wash my hands it was so cold that it felt like my hands were frozen. After that my hands hurt. And I'm not the only one. I saw a kid who didn't wash his hands. He must have been too cold. Even though the school may be trying to save money, I think no hot water in the sinks makes us not want to wash our hands.

In order to kill germs, you have to use hot water when you wash your hands and do the dishes. Germs can live in the cold water, so you have to use hot to kill them. When I wash my hands in cold water, even if I use soap some of the germs can stick around. What's the point of washing then? Aren't we just going to get sick anyway? Maybe the school is worried we are going to burn ourselves with hot water. But don't they want us to be healthy and not sick?

Maybe we should raise the extra money for the school to pay for the hot water. That way we will feel more important. We will have hot water to wash our hands on cold days. And we will kill germs when we wash.

—Kim T., Helen K., Joanne L., and Pilar M.

Vocabulary Tone

Objective

The student will recognize and utilize appropriate diction to add precision and interest to written work.

Skills

—analyzing writing for connotation in word choice
—using lively and vivid words in writing
—utilizing precise words to add to the reader's understanding

Materials

—student copies of "*Harry Potter and the Prisoner of Azkaban*" (page 80)
—student copies of "The Tone of Vocabulary" (page 81)
—writing paper
—student writing sample on page 82 (for teacher reference)

Procedure

1. Distribute copies of "*Harry Potter and the Prisoner of Azkaban*" to the students. Read the article aloud as a class.

2. As the students read, point out the places where the author's ideas appeal to readers due to the word choice.

3. Introduce the concept of connotation to students. Connotations are the images and associations a word has beyond its literal, dictionary definition. For example, a house simply suggests the dwelling a person lives in, but a mansion suggests that the house is unusually large and stately.

4. Be sure students have identified the author's use of descriptive words that help create a positive attitude toward the book. First, Rowling has "enchanted" readers with her "finely crafted" works. The third book is "irresistible."

5. Distribute copies of "The Tone of Vocabulary" to the students. Have them work independently to complete the activity page.

6. Review the students' answers with the class. Be sure to define any words that students do not know. This is also a good opportunity to review synonyms for the words on the list.

7. When students are finished, you may wish to have them work in pairs to develop other pairs of words that differ in connotation.

8. Instruct each student to write a paragraph about something he or she either likes or dislikes. Each student should focus on using the connotation of words to appeal to the readers.

Vocabulary Tone *(cont.)*

Publication

1. Ask students to volunteer to read their paragraphs aloud to the class. While volunteers are reading, have the rest of the students make a list of the words that stand out as interesting, powerful, lively, or particularly precise. The writer will find this exercise especially helpful. Students can also make vocabulary suggestions to the writer. Students may wish to rewrite their paragraphs after this activity.

2. Ask students to underline or highlight the words they have selected in their writing to add precision, interest, or power. Post the finished paragraphs on a bulletin board in the classroom.

Extension

1. Provide students with enough time to peruse a dictionary and thesaurus by giving them a word hunt to complete in class. Set a time limit and choose a theme in advance. Have students work in teams to find words that relate to the theme. Remember, the goal is to find new vocabulary and more precise language.

2. Have students find at least two examples of writings in which the author uses connotation. Create a class book of the examples.

Harry Potter and the Prisoner of Azkaban

J.K. Rowling burst on the literary scene in 1997 with her first book, *Harry Potter and the Sorcerer's Stone.* She has enchanted readers around the world with her finely crafted works of fantasy and adventure. *Harry Potter and the Prisoner of Azkaban,* the third in the series, follows the further adventures of a young wizard-in-training. If you haven't been introduced to Harry Potter, go directly to a bookstore or library and correct that mistake. If you have, you will be happy to hear that the latest volume is as irresistible as the first two.

In the first book, readers were introduced to Harry Potter, who at ten learns he is, in fact, the orphan son of a wizard and a witch. His parents were murdered by a wicked wizard named Voldemort, and Potter has been raised by an aunt and uncle without a drop of magic in their blood. The first book and the second, *Harry Potter and the Chamber of Secrets*, describe Potter's first two years at Hogwarts School of Witchcraft and Wizardry. There, Potter attended intriguing classes such as Defense Against the Dark Arts. At the same time, he becomes involved in amazing adventures and excels at Quidditch. What, you ask, is Quidditch? It's a sport combining elements of soccer, cricket, and jousting and played by people on flying broomsticks.

The books themselves have been flying off the shelves of bookstores as eager fans, bewitched by Rowling's talent, rush to read her latest work. Why is everyone so wild about Harry?

Rowling has created a winning mix of magic and everyday elements. So far in her series, she has found inventive ways to serve up classic fantasy. At Hogwarts, owls deliver mail, paintings talk, and ghosts drift the halls. A really good book needs a winning hero, and Rowling has invented a winner in Harry Potter. He is flawed enough to be real, but courageous and smart enough to be heroic. The supporting characters are interesting and original, as well. Add suspense and high adventure and you have all the necessary ingredients to keep the reader glued to the story.

Harry Potter and the Prisoner of Azkaban is yet another example of this winning mix. Harry learns that Sirius Black, a treacherous wizard who once killed thirteen people with a single curse, has escaped from the fortress prison of Azkaban and is after Harry. "Dementors"—beings who can suck out a person's soul—are sent to guard Hogwarts and protect Harry from Black. But they become more threat than help, as they trap people into thinking of their most horrible memories. The plot thickens, suspense builds, and Rowling adds more twists and turns to this magic world she has created. It's a world you won't want to miss!

The Tone of Vocabulary

Below you will find pairs of words grouped together. The definitions of the word pairs are essentially the same, but one of the words carries a more negative connotation. Circle the word that you think is more negative of the two.

Example:

stately	observer
gigantic	inspector
opinionated	tyrant
assertive	ruler
cottage	companion
hovel	bosom buddy
submissive	persistent
weak	stubborn
resistant	frigid
stubborn	cold
skinny	eat
slender	devour
used	short
pre-owned	petite
messy	reduce
disorderly	cut back
colorful	curious
tacky	nosy
old	old
vintage	mature
strict	pungent
orderly	fragrant

Student Writing Sample

My Brother

My brother is a trouble-maker because he is always spying on me and trying to find out what I do so that he can tell on me. He is nosy and always asks me what I am doing. Sometimes I find him in my room rifling through my things. He has eyes like a badger because he is always hunting around for something.

—Jill L.

Active Verbs

Objective

The student will replace static verbs with lively verbs to strengthen written work.

Skills

—brainstorming action verbs

—understanding the use of action verbs

—understanding that passive verbs weaken writing

—using active verbs in order to enliven writing

—using active verbs in the writing of paragraphs and essays

Materials

—sheets of paper

—chalkboard or overhead projector

—student copies of "Cup of Poison" (page 85)

—writing paper

—student writing sample on page 86 (for teacher reference)

Procedure

1. Ask students to brainstorm and record lists of action verbs with partners.

2. When the students are finished, write all of the verbs on the chalkboard for the entire class to see.

3. Explain to the students that verbs that convey an action help the reader to visualize what is happening in a narrative or expository essay. On the other hand, passive verbs are static and weaken the overall effectiveness of the written work.

4. Distribute copies of "Cup of Poison" to the students. Read the article aloud to the class, and ask students to underline the active verbs used that enliven the writing. After reading the article, ask students to review their underlined words as a class.

5. Ask students to work with partners to create five sentences that utilize active verbs. Ask students to avoid using passive constructions in their sentences.

6. Have students present their two best sentences to the class by writing them on the chalkboard, on an overhead, or by reading them aloud.

7. Allow the class to vote on the two best sentences presented (not necessarily from the same pair of students) and ask them to write paragraphs using one of the sentences and using active verbs.

Active Verbs *(cont.)*

Publication

1. Because the students will be using one of two sentences, many of the paragraphs will have similar themes. Invite the students to read their paragraphs aloud to the class.

2. Have the students compare and contrast the verbs and themes presented.

3. Create an active verb Web site for your class on which you post some or all of the paragraphs for the students to view. (Be sure to obtain permission to post student work on the Internet. Also, in order to ensure student safety, be sure to monitor Internet use or convey to parents the importance of monitoring their children's use of the Internet.)

Extension

1. Ask the students to create essays from their paragraphs, focusing on the use of active verbs throughout their writing.

2. Have students take previously written essays and rewrite them by focusing their attention on the use of active verbs.

3. Find examples of writing in which the use of passive verbs weakens the story or argument. Make these available to the students for their reading.

4. Make an active verb wall in your classroom where students can write interesting and useful active verbs that they find while they are reading.

Cup of Poison

In its raucous heyday 80 years ago, Butte, Montana, was known as the richest hill on earth. Its rocky soil yielded millions of tons of copper ore, used to make the wires that spread power and light and phones across the nation. Then, 16 years ago, the giant strip mine was closed, and the pumps that kept it dry were turned off for good.

Ever since, waters from the surrounding bedrock and from a maze of old mind tunnels and shafts have been rushing in and reacting with the ores to form a toxic soup that rises steadily, year after year, like water in a vast bathtub. It's the Berkeley Pit, an oval lake of acidic mining residues so deep that it could swallow an 80-story skyscraper.

Townsfolk celebrate this strange monument, which, deceptively green and picturesque, sparkles on postcards. The Chamber of Commerce runs a trolley to the viewing stand and gift shop that operates high over the waters. But even as visitors stream in, authorities must take elaborate steps to scare away waterfowl with loudspeakers, firecrackers, and a boat. Such precautions weren't in place three years ago, when migrating Canadian snow geese had the misfortune to touchdown on the waters for a drink. In the following days, officials encountered 342 carcasses floating and washed ashore, their insides scoured with burns and sores.

Now those rising waters—26 billion gallons—lap menacingly just blocks from the center of town and 360 ft. below the rim of the pit, threatening one day to spill into an underground aquifer and send a tide of contaminants seeping into neighborhoods and creeks across the Summit Valley.

To remove and treat the poisons before they reach the danger level, some residents propose mining the Berkeley lake. There is growing talk of seeking to extract perhaps hundreds of millions of dollars worth of zinc, copper, magnesium and other minerals that lie dissolved in the waters.

ARCO and Montana Resources, the pit's custodians, like the idea of mining the fetid lake. But a local environmental firm says a workable process could be years off. That's too long to wait, critics warn. A disturbing reading in one of 42 monitoring wells surrounding the lake suggests a possible reversal of seepage. Instead of flowing toward the pit, the water may be heading away from it.

The U.S. Environmental Protection Agency and Montana officials insist that years before the danger level could be reached, some solution—treating the mess or mining it—will be in place to halt the lake's rise. But Butte's destiny, as has happened before, will ultimately be decided by outside forces. Congress is currently trying to piece together a new Superfund law designed to force polluters to bear the cost of cleaning up toxic sites. That law could determine how fast—or how slowly—the cleanup of Montana's newest, deepest lake proceeds.

Student Writing Sample

Active Verbs Assignment

Two sentences:

- The disgusting fly buzzed in the air, irritating everyone.

- The small boy secretly dashed around the corner to avoid the bully.

Everyone always picked on him. They clucked at him like chickens. They even barked at him like dogs. He just hid in the shadows, hoping to avoid everyone. But the school bully hunted after him that day. Luckily, the boy spied the bully early on. The small boy secretly dashed around the corner to avoid the bully. He hid himself away until the moment passed.

—Hunter B.

Synonyms

Objective

The student will pay close attention to word choice to add precision to written work.

Skills

—choosing words that are specific and accurate for writing

—selecting words and phrases that help the reader create mental images while reading

Materials

—overhead transparency of "Hunting: Are Kids Caught in the Line of Fire?" (page 89)

—overhead projector

—student copies of "Writing Synonyms" (page 90)

—writing paper

—red or green pens

—student writing sample on page 91 (for teacher reference)

Procedure

1. Display the overhead transparency of "Hunting: Are Kids Caught in the Line of Fire?" Have students take turns reading the article aloud.

2. Ask students to find five different places in the article where they believe the author precisely chose a specific word to help create a more accurate mental image for the reader.

3. Have students share the five words they have chosen, and ask them to defend their choices by listing less effective words the author probably avoided.

4. Distribute copies of "Writing Synonyms" to the students. You may choose to allow the use of a thesaurus or rely on their own vocabulary for the exercise.

5. As an alternative, make a competition out of it by placing the students in teams of two and giving them a time limit to come up with the longest list of words. If you chose to not use a thesaurus for the activity, it would be wise to supplement the students with the information from the thesaurus.

6. Review the lists with the entire class and require students to add words to their lists that they neglected.

7. Have each student select a vague topic to write about, such as the big house. Require the students to use precise word choice in order to help the reader visualize the scene with clear pictures in their minds.

Synonyms *(cont.)*

Publication

1. Have students exchange their paragraphs with one another. Ask the students to use colored pens (red or green) to underline the places where they believe the writers have chosen precise, specific words that help create more accurate visual images.

2. Place the finished paragraphs on a bulletin board in the classroom and allow time for the students to view them and read them.

3. Have students provide illustrations or storyboards for their paragraphs. Create a class book of the illustrations and the paragraphs, copy them, and distribute to each of the students.

Extension

1. Provide students with many examples of writing in which the author has carefully chosen his or her words to strengthen the piece. Underline the effective words for the students or ask them to identify the words.

2. Find a model of good writing and ask students to write synonyms for words that you underline. Ask them to choose one of the words they have listed and explain how it would change the paragraph if the author had chosen to use it.

3. Provide students with "holey essays" (essays in which you omit key words and phrases). Ask students to fill in the blanks using precise word choice.

Hunting: Are Kids Caught in the Line of Fire?

Dear Editors,

I am the proud mother of a 16-year-old hunter named Melissa. We live in rural Maryland. This year, the 250,000 whitetail deer in our state will cause $38 million in crop damage and nearly $10 million in other property damage.

Urban sprawl is gobbling up the natural environments of the deer. Without plants to eat, hundreds of thousands of deer are starving to death—a slow, painful process. These spreaders of Lyme disease stumble onto our highways, searching for food and causing countless car wrecks. In my opinion, hunting acts as the most humane form of population control by quickly reducing the numbers of suffering animals.

Hunters are trained to respect the powerful dignity of animals and their environment. I didn't just push my daughter into a field and say, "Okay. Shoot!" As in nearly every other state, Melissa had to attend a thorough training program in order to get her hunting license. The focus wasn't just on guns and how to shoot, but also on the morality of hunting and how to be sensitive to the fragility of nature.

According to the FBI Academy in Quantico, Virginia, there is no evidence that shows that kids who hunt grow up to be violent adults. If anything, these kids learn respect for guns—that they are powerful weapons, not toys.

I have told Melissa, "Shoot only what you plan to eat." Nothing is wasted. What other sport can teach children such respect and restraint?

Sincerely,
Alice Weisman
Middletown, Maryland

Dear Editors,

What do hunters think on a beautiful fall morning? "Ah, the sun is shining, the birds are chirping. Gosh, I can't wait to blow away that deer!" How does destroying part of nature bring you closer to nature?

Many people complain that we have lost touch with nature because we buy meat in plastic-safe packaging at the grocery store. News flash: This is not a bad thing. It's called progress. Rather than spending all of our time gathering food, we can work on advancing ourselves.

People who call hunting a sport are confused. What is the key element in athletics? Sportsmanship. Every year, American hunters kill 200,000,000 defenseless animals, using superior weaponry. It's like using a tank to serve a ball in tennis. If you want meat so badly, go to a fast-food store and order a cheeseburger. That certainly seems a lot more sportsmanlike than blowing away Bambi's mother.

And hunters use satellite-guided, global-positioning systems and night-vision binoculars to track and murder. Where is the skill—or the sport—in flicking buttons and following blips on a screen?

Hunters are quick to point out that hunting has fewer accidents than boating. Tell that comforting fact to the 13-year-old Wisconsin boy who accidentally shot and killed another hunter. At least in water skiing, other skiers don't shoot you.

The gun makers send videotapes and other materials to our schools. Why? Money. If you hook a kid at twelve and he hunts until he's sixty, you've sold him a lot of guns and ammo during his lifetime.

Just like tobacco and alcohol, hunting is a drug. Think about it. Because you better believe that the gun makers are.

Yours in Peace,
Nathan Moore
Petersburg, Virginia

Writing Synonyms

Sometimes in writing, you will want to use a word but it doesn't sound quite right. Using a thesaurus in these instances can be helpful. Beside each word below, write a list of all of the synonyms you can think of or that you find in a thesaurus.

1. house

_____

_____

2. fat

_____

_____

3. skinny

_____

_____

4. hurt

_____

_____

5. mad

_____

_____

6. strange

_____

_____

7. nice

_____

_____

8. loud

_____

_____

9. happy

_____

_____

10. sad

_____

_____

Student Writing Sample

Creature on the Hill

(Inspired by *Shrek* by William Steig, my little brother's favorite book)

On top of the hill sat a horrible ogre. His green skin was covered in boils and puss-filled sores. He didn't have any hair because it all fell out when he was born. His bloodshot eyes boiled with anger and he could shoot out laser beams from them and burn things. People ran away when they smelled his breath because it made them gasp for air.

—Gracen A.

Puns

Objective

The student will use precise word choice and figurative language to enrich writing.

Skills

—using puns to enliven the language of writing
—using puns to lighten the tone of writing

Materials

—overhead transparency of "Bats in the Ball Park" (page 94)
—overhead projector
—student copies of "Fun with Puns" (page 95)
—writing paper
—student writing sample on page 96 (for teacher reference)

Procedure

1. Ask students if they know what a pun is. Try to guide them to come up with the response.

2. If no one in the class knows, enlist the help of a student to look up the definition of pun in the dictionary. This will emphasize to the class that they can find information without their teacher as a guide.

3. Supplement their understanding of puns by explaining that most puns are based on the use of a single word that generates two different meanings. There are two types of puns—homographic and homophonic puns. Homographic puns are created when two meanings spring from the same spelling. If the spelling differs according to each meaning, then the pun is homophonic.

4. Place the overhead transparency of "Bats in the Ball Park" on the overhead projector and read the article aloud to the students.

5. Ask students to look for the puns in the article. Have them identify the type of pun— homographic or homophonic.

6. Discuss the effect of using puns (or a play on words) in writing. Because puns are a play on words, they usually cause writing to become more light-hearted and funny. Essentially, puns are jokes.

7. Ask the students to identify other places in the article where the author utilizes a light-hearted tone through word choice.

8. Distribute copies of "Fun with Puns" to the students. Ask students to work in pairs to complete the activity page. This can be a difficult task for even the strongest of writers, so be encouraging. Students may need more space to provide background for their puns. Be sure to review the answers with the class to check for understanding.

Puns *(cont.)*

9. Have each student write a paragraph in which he or she uses a pun to lighten the tone. A pun could also be used as the title. Leave the topic open so the student can have the room to create an original and effective pun.

Publication

1. Allow the students to create a humor newspaper for the class in which they can print their original puns and other humorous writings.

2. Duplicate the newspaper and distribute copies to the students. They will enjoy reading the paper for years to come.

Extension

1. Ask students to bring in at least two examples of puns from newspapers and magazines.

2. Display the examples on the bulletin board in the classroom. Advise students that puns are commonly found in titles of articles.

3. Ask students to watch television for examples of puns. Ask them to find one example from television or the movies. Encourage them to look at not only the content of the puns, but the overall effect on the program or movie.

Bats in the Ball Park

It's a pretty sure bet that where there's a baseball team there are bats. But in 1998, the New York Mets found themselves with nearly 30,000 bats to spare. These bats were not made of wood or aluminum—they were alive and flapping! The team's spring-training stadium in Port St. Lucie, Florida, was home to a colony of Brazilian free-tailed bats. That spring, a special "bat house" opened near the stadium. Its builders hope the bats will move in and leave the Mets alone.

Time out! How did thousands of furry bats end up in a baseball stadium? Throughout Florida, new buildings are replacing the forests where bats usually live. "Bats are being forced to live closer and closer to people," says University of Florida wildlife expert Ken Gioeli (Joe-ell-ee).

Too close, say the Mets. The team was fed up with its winged fans. Not only were the bats giving people the creeps, but they were also leaving a giant mess. In one night, 30,000 bats can produce several inches of droppings, which are called guano (gwah-no). The health department's officials were worried. Catsup and mustard are fine on a hot dog, but an accidental helping of guano? Yecch!

The bats had to go. But killing bats is illegal in Florida. They are a protected species. So one night while the bats were out, special screening was put up to keep them from returning to the stadium. Result: a lot of homeless bats.

Now that Gioeli's specially designed bat house is open, many of those bats will soon have a home. That's good news for the bats and for local farmers, too. Not only do bats eat pesky insects, but the guano from the new bat house can be used as fertilizer to help crops grow. Says Gioeli: "It's very rich in nutrients."

Fun with Puns

On the back of this paper, write an explanation of one of the puns from "Bats in the Ball Park" to your reader. Pretend your reader is a foreigner who doesn't understand the meaning of the pun.

Below you will find words that can be used to create simple puns. With a partner, create as many puns as you can with the words below.

Example: see/sea   I'm on a seafood diet; whenever I see food, I eat it.

  1. red/read

  _____

  2. close/clothes

  _____

  3. ant/aunt

  _____

  4. ate/eight

  _____

  5. hole/whole

  _____

  6. deck/deck

  _____

  7. capital/capitol

  _____

  8. principal/principle

  _____

  9. bye/buy

  _____

  10. fly/fly

  _____

  11. blew/blue

  _____

  12. feet/feat

  _____

  13. sail/sale

  _____

  14. bee/be

  _____

Student Writing Sample

My Bedroom

My bedroom is very messy. I don't like cleaning much because I think cleaning is boring. I get yelled at a lot because I don't clean my room enough. My mom says that my room is a pigsty, but I say it is a pig's sigh. It is so comfortable and cozy that if a pig saw it, he would sigh with happiness. He would fall back into my pile of dirty clothes and go to sleep.

—*Jordan T.*

Pronouns

Objective

The student will recognize and write sentences using pronouns that are clear and easy to understand.

Skills

—identifying clear and unclear pronoun references in sentences

—writing sentences with clear pronoun references to achieve greater understanding for the reader

Materials

—chalkboard

—overhead transparency of "Class Without Boys" (page 99)

—overhead projector

—student copies of "Pronoun Reference and Consistency" (page 100)

—blank overhead transparencies

—wipe-off markers

—writing paper

—student writing sample on page 101 (for teacher reference)

Procedure

1. Begin the lesson by reviewing the purpose of pronouns in speech and in writing. Pronouns are used to reduce repetition because repeating the same noun over and over again can weaken the effectiveness of writing.

2. Place the following sentences on the chalkboard (excluding those in parentheses):

   —From where I was standing, you could see the Brooklyn Bridge. (*From where I was standing, I could see the Brooklyn Bridge.*)

   —In the newspaper it said that you should eat 5–7 servings of fruits and vegetables a day. (*The newspaper said that you should eat 5–7 servings of fruits and vegetables a day.*)

   —Whenever Kelly races Connie on her scooter, she always wins. (*Connie always wins whenever she and Kelly race on their scooters.*)

   —A person should study if they want to succeed in life. (*A person should study if he or she wants to succeed in life or people should study if they want to succeed in life.*)

3. Divide the students into groups of two. Have them work together to identify the pronoun problems in the sentences.

4. After the students are finished working, have students stand at the chalkboard and present their findings to the class. Follow up after each presentation by explaining how the sentences should be corrected to make them more clear to the reader.

Pronouns *(cont.)*

5. Display the overhead transparency of "Class Without Boys" and review the use of pronoun reference and consistency. Look at the sentence, "Roughly speaking, until they reach their teens, American girls outperform boys." The sentence is structured so that girls appears closest to the pronoun *their*, making the pronoun reference clear to the reader. Another strategy the author uses is to make the nouns plural. For example, in the sentence, "While boys and girls in these single-sex academies spent most of the day apart, they mixed during one or two elective periods and socialized during lunch." The word *they* refers to both boys and girls. Had the sentence been written about a single boy or girl, it might have been more confusing for the reader.

6. Distribute copies of "Pronoun Reference and Consistency" to the students. Ask them to complete the activity independently.

7. When students have completed the activity, distribute blank transparencies and markers to them. Assign them each a number, and have them write their response on the transparency. Have the students present their results to the class. Because the students may have different answers, it is a good idea to have more than one of them do each number.

8. Ask each student to write a brief essay about whether or not he or she believes girls and boys should attend same-sex schools. Have the students pay close attention to the use of pronouns, and have the student underline all pronouns and the nouns to which they refer.

Publication

Allow students to have a class debate about same-sex education. Allow students to use the information and support presented in the paragraphs to help make their case. If some students will not be participating in the presentation of materials, have them take notes and keep track of the evidence. Allow them to vote to determine the winner.

Extension

1. Encourage students to develop a keen ear for poor pronoun consistency and reference by making an effort to point out errors found in print and in speech. With every error found, ask students to come up with a better and more precise replacement sentence.

2. Collect examples of poor pronoun reference and inconsistencies from the students' writings. Make a worksheet of the errors and allow the class to correct the errors.

Class Without Boys

In Elaine Lewinnek's all-girl sixth grade social-studies class, the Venus of Willendorf's bulging stomach and hips were a hot topic. A picture of the fertility goddess from 25,000 B.C. stimulated a lively discussion about how ideals of feminine beauty have changed through the centuries. Then a boy came into the classroom to collect attendance slips. "Stop! Stop! There's a boy in the room!" several girls shouted. The conversation halted until he left.

To Lewinnek, it was a clear demonstration of how girls may learn better without boys. Marina Middle School in San Francisco, where Lewinnek teaches, is one of only a handful of U.S. public schools that are trying single-sex education for some students.

It's too early to pass judgment. But already the teachers are enthusiastic. So are their female pupils. "If there were boys, I'd be scared to talk out," says 12-year-old Genora Turner. "I'm learning better in this all-girl class."

That is exactly what single-sex advocates expected to hear. Roughly speaking, until they reach their teens, American girls outperform boys. Then something changes, and boys push ahead, especially in science. Whether the cause is bias, genes, or some combination, no one knows for sure. But if you can just keep the sexes apart for a while, the theory goes, girls at least may benefit. "It's good to have a safe place without the distraction of the opposite sex," says Lewinnek.

Encouraged by a few studies supporting the idea, Marina Middle School principal John Michealson organized all-girl and all-boy classes for the first time last year. Marina doesn't segregate girls and boys into separate schools or even separate buildings. In fact, only about 105 of Marina's 810 students are separated so far; the rest attend typical coed classes. Michaelson started the single-sex experiment by setting aside two rooms—one for 30 seventh-grade boys and one for 30 seventh-grade girls. While boys and girls in the single-sex "academies" spent most of the day apart, they mixed during one or two elective periods and socialized during lunch. "This way the kids get the best of both," says Michaelson.

Though the seventh-graders in Marina's single-sex program had the option of switching to coed classes, few did. At year's end the results were encouraging. "In general, their attention was more on their academic activities," says Lorraine Perry, 50, who taught science and math in both single-sex academies last year. As Perry hoped, the girls flourished away from male competition. The surprise was that boys thrived, too. "They were a little more open," says Perry, "to admitting that they didn't understand something than if there had been girls in class."

San Francisco hopes to continue its program at least through next year. "I think we're compelled to come up with a variety of choices for students and families," says Michaelson. "It's arrogant to assume that any student is going to learn in a standard way." Schools that separate boys from girls will not help every distracted student, but they may be the answer for some."

Pronouns Reference and Consistency

First, identify the lack of clarity in the following sentences. Then, correct any problems with unclear pronoun reference or pronoun consistency by rewriting the sentence.

1. My father is an engineer, but I am not interested in it.

   Problem: _____

   Correct: _____

2. Whenever Sarah goes over to Soraya's house, she always makes popcorn.

   Problem: _____

   Correct: _____

3. During Michael Jordan's press conference, he announced his return to professional basketball.

   Problem: _____

   Correct: _____

4. An onion fell to the floor just as I was about to chop it apart.

   Problem: _____

   Correct: _____

5. I have had a cold for the last two weeks which really makes me mad.

   Problem: _____

   Correct: _____

6. On television last night, they said that there was a bad accident on the freeway.

   Problem: _____

   Correct: _____

7. In most buildings it says "No Smoking."

   Problem: _____

   Correct: _____

8. Tonya got married three years ago, and it is still going strong.

   Problem: _____

   Correct: _____

9. When a person is learning how to snowboard, they fall a lot at first.

   Problem: _____

   Correct: _____

10. Criminals are never smart about the crimes they commit. He leaves lots of evidence, and he always gives himself away during the interrogation. They usually get caught.

    Problem: _____

    Correct: _____

Student Writing Sample

An All-Girl School

    I don't like going to school with boys. I wish I went to a school with only girls. Boys make going to school harder because they tease girls and don't let them play sports all the time. I would like to go to a school where only girls go because I think I would do better in my classes. Sometimes boys yell out the answers before I've even had a chance to think about the question. I think boys make the class louder and if our class didn't have them it would be quieter. I think girls are afraid to talk out in class because they worry about what the boys are thinking. If there were no boys, the girls would talk out more.

—Shira E.

Adjectives

Objective

The student will examine and utilize vivid adjectives to enrich writing.

Skills

—examining the use of vivid adjectives to enrich writing

—utilizing vivid adjectives to enrich writing

Materials

—overhead transparency of "How the Vikings Lived" (page 104)

—overhead projector

—writing paper

—index cards

—marker

—highlighter pens

—student writing sample on page 105 (for teacher reference)

Procedure

1. Display the overhead transparency of "How the Vikings Lived" and, as you read the article aloud to the class, ask students to silently identify the adjectives. If students need instruction in how to identify adjectives, it may be a good idea to begin with a brief reminder about how adjectives work in a sentence.

2. Ask each student to write down five examples of adjectives they find in the article.

3. Ask the class if the use of adjectives helps the reader of the article to see pictures or understand the author's point better.

4. After learning about adjectives, have students play a game (in groups of three) and compete to see which group can describe an item with the greatest number of adjectives in the shortest period of time.

5. Prepare a stack of index cards by using a marker to print the name of a different noun on each one. You will want each group to have the same nouns to work with. Examples: house, car, fence, school, store, motorcycle, train, cake, etc. You will want enough cards for each group of three students to have up to ten cards, depending how many times you want to perform the activity.

6. As you distribute the cards to each group, place them facedown so that students cannot look at the words. Give the groups a limited amount of time to work on each word.

7. At the end of the brainstorming period in which students have written down their adjectives, make a list of the words all of the groups have created and record them on the chalkboard.

Adjectives *(cont.)*

8. Keep the list of adjectives for each noun on the chalkboard for the class to see throughout the game. Any word that has been used by more than one group does not receive points. For each unique adjective the groups present, they earn one point. Provide the winning group with a prize.

9. Ask each student to write a paragraph about any of the nouns used in the game, using any of the adjectives presented by the class. Encourage the student to add additional adjectives to his or her paragraph that were not presented.

Publication

1. Allow students to read their paragraphs aloud to the class. Ask the rest of the students to close their eyes and attempt to visualize the item as the reader describes it.

2. Have students exchange paragraphs with a partner. Have the students use highlighter pens to identify the adjectives used in the paragraph.

Extension

1. Ask students to bring in at least two examples of published writing that contain worthwhile adjectives. Require them to identify the adjectives. Make a book of all of the writings to keep in the class library.

2. When writing about a specific topic or, for example, a character in a novel, use the game to allow students to brainstorm for their essays. When they have a large vocabulary and a number of ideas with which to work, their essays will be much better.

How the Vikings Lived

Greenland is not very green at all. Most of the world's largest island is frozen, buried beneath endless fields of snow.

More than a thousand years ago, Erik the Red, a Viking explorer, left his home in Iceland and discovered a rich supply of fish, whale, walrus, and seal in uninhabited Greenland's waters. But he needed help to harvest the riches. He guessed that an attractive name might lure fellow Vikings from their cold homeland to an even colder place. So he called the new land Greenland.

Some Vikings must have been tricked by the name. About 5,000 of them packed up longships and made the dangerous crossing. Warriors and tradesmen began exploring. Families set up homes along the narrow inlets, called fjords (fee-yords).

TREASURES IN THE SAND

Like a freezer, Greenland's cold climate has preserved traces of these ancient settlements. Scientists thought they had found them all until 1992, when Inuit (In-oo-it) hunters stumbled across some unusual pieces of wood floating into a fjord near the capital city of Nuuk. They had found a lost Viking settlement.

Now a team of archaeologists from around the world has finished the painstaking job of exploring it. Known as the "village beneath the sand," the settlement was actually a large farm where Vikings lived for more than 300 years. Six buildings of stone and peat (rotted moss and other plants) had up to 30 rooms each.

Digging through ancient storerooms and kitchens, the scientists found a treasure chest of Viking daily life: kitchen utensils, walrus-tooth dice, and reindeer-bone necklaces. Miniature boats and wooden boxes may have been children's toys. "It was a hard life," says Danish archaeologist Jette Arneborg, "but not without its comforts."

Why was the farm abandoned? Viking colonies began disappearing from Greenland in the 1300s. Arneborg suggests that "the weather got worse and trade dried up. Europe was no longer interested in the materials Greenland could provide."

DID YOU KNOW?

- Vikings probably got their name from the Old Norse verb *vika*, which means "to go off." They left their homes in Scandinavia to trade—and raid—in Europe from about 800 to 1100.

- Vikings treasured their fierce weapons. They gave the heavy swords, spearheads, and battle-axes nicknames like "Leg Biter" and "Long and Sharp."

- Vikings wore helmets with horns not during battle, but during prayer to gods like Thor, the god of thunder. They wore thin leather caps for war.

- Vikings wrote by inscribing words on stone, using an ancient and mysterious system of letters and symbols called runes.

- Viking ships had a high prow (front) and high stern (back) for smoother rides in rough seas. Heroes were buried in huge graves with their ships; it was believed that they would sail on in the afterworld.

Student Writing Sample

Descriptive Writing

Topic: house

Adjectives: big, dark, ancient, new, expansive, lonely, expensive, gloomy, old, painted, cozy, comfortable, showy, practical, deserted, empty, creepy, ugly, inviting, ranch, little, filthy, country, dirty, eerie, model, unique, rare, excellent, crowded, busy, welcoming, warm, neat, clean, attractive, pretty, wood, mobile, mansion, country, drooping

The big, dark mansion house sits alone at the end of the cul-de-sac. It is an ancient country house that is really expensive but now it is just deserted. It has a lonely look about it, with the trees drooping down in the front yard like they are crying. The paint is old and has peeled off. The front door has a creepy and ugly knocker on it that really makes the house seem showy but eerie at the same time. A long time ago the house might have been inviting and warm, but today it is filthy and dirty with cobwebs and dust because it is empty.

—Justine C.

Description

Objective

The student will use specific and concrete words to appeal to the senses in descriptive writing.

Skills

—providing details and sensory description to enliven writing
—replacing trite expressions with vivid description

Materials

—student copies of "Adding Description" (page 108)
—overhead transparency of "Race the Wind" (page 109)
—overhead projector
—index cards (each printed with a different student's name)
—writing paper
—envelopes
—small strips of paper
—student copies of "Eliminating Clichés" (page 110)
—student writing sample on page 111 (for teacher reference)

Procedure

1. When introducing the descriptive voice to students, it is helpful to illustrate the difference between cold, hard facts and the use of descriptive details that can appeal to the reader's emotions and senses. The difference between "She is beautiful" and "Her brilliant green eyes dramatically glare at you underneath her glossy black hair," is that we can understand the concrete details that are present in the second sentence, while the first sentence remains too vague and abstract for us to completely understand. It is the difference between showing and telling in writing.

2. Distribute copies of "Adding Description" to the students. Allow them to work in pairs or independently to complete the activity page.

3. Invite students to share their sentences with the class and encourage the rest of the students to attempt to visualize the scenes. Be sure to remind students that too much description is a waste of effort. All description must be purposeful and relevant. For example, if a student is writing a description of meat, it does not matter what the meat smells like if it is the appearance to which the writer is reacting.

4. Display the overhead transparency of "Race the Wind" on the overhead projector and read the article to the class.

5. As you read, ask students to point out to the class the places where the author uses description to help add to the mood, contribute to the suspense, to paint the scene.

Description *(cont.)*

6. Discuss the effectiveness of the description in the article. What is the author's purpose? How does the use of description help her achieve her purpose? Point out that the author does not use trite or overused phrases (called clichés). This is important because clichés detract from the effectiveness of the description because they are too predictable. It is much more effective for students to use their own original comparisons in their writing.

7. Place the names of the students on index cards, mix them up and distribute them to the class. Have each student write a complimentary description of the person named on the card. Advise them to use the descriptions to support a main idea. For example, "Cathy is very friendly," is a main idea that can be supported by details about her smiling eyes, inviting grin, and pleasant personality.

Publication

1. Invite each student to read the description aloud to the person about whom they wrote. You may also want to post the descriptions without naming the subject on a bulletin board and invite students to peruse them and guess who the subject is. Post an envelope below each description and allow students to place the names of their guess on a piece of paper in the envelope.

2. Assemble a class album featuring each description and a photo of the student.

Extension

1. Distribute copies of "Eliminating Clichés" to the students. Have them work independently to complete the activity page. Review their responses as a class.

2. Have students bring in examples of articles that contain particularly effective and vivid descriptions. Allow students to imitate the descriptions by creating a structured form in which you eliminate some of the key words.

3. Allow students to spend time outside observing nature and have them write detailed descriptions of their time outdoors.

Adding Description

Rewrite the following simple phrases using vivid and descriptive details.

Example: Jack was sick.

Rewrite: Jack, a young child of two, suffered terribly with his first sinus infection. He looked more like Rudolph than a little tot with his swollen, red nose, and his cough made him sound more like an old hag on the verge of her death.

1. It was raining.

_____

_____

2. John was tired.

_____

_____

3. It was cold.

_____

_____

4. A car drove by.

_____

_____

5. A cat sat at the window.

_____

_____

6. It was hot.

_____

_____

7. She felt nervous.

_____

_____

8. She looked beautiful.

_____

_____

9. The house stood empty.

_____

_____

10. The movie began.

_____

_____

Race the Wind

When the sands began kicking up and lashing our faces, I started to worry that maybe we had made a mistake. Maybe we should have left the beach.

That afternoon, my dad had stood on the deck of our home and laughed as our neighbors packed up their cars and headed inland. They left to spend the night in motels or at friends' homes that were out of range of the approaching summer storm. My dad believed his family was made of stronger stuff.

Challenging the weather to dampen our spirits, my sister, my mom, and I lit a fire on the beach. Dad told jokes, using stick skewers to cook up marshmallows that tasted like burnt bark.

Now, it was 6:30 p.m. and all the laughter evaporated. Our eyes were drawn to the sky. A dark wall of clouds marched toward us. The red sunset bled through the storm clouds, turning the sky into a swirling torrent of dark fire. Below, the black waves of Lake Michigan grappled and slammed against each other as they sent icy tendrils toward the sky. Both sky and lake appeared locked in a dangerous battle and we were trapped in the middle.

"Look!" My sister, Kim, spotted it first. Her tiny finger pointed toward the horizon. It was a waterspout—a tornado whose funnel was made of fresh water—and it was heading straight for us.

In a flash, we were all on our feet. My dad began mumbling, "It's okay, it's okay." The wind started screaming and now we were running toward the cottage. My mom stopped next to the front door. "Where can we go?" She shouted the question at my dad.

Most cottages on this part of Lake Michigan had been built without basements—and ours was no exception. The huge bay windows and rickety construction of the cottage interior wouldn't offer safety from high winds.

I turned to look at the sky. Now it didn't look beautiful. It looked deadly. This liquid sister of the tornado wouldn't wait for us to get in the car and drive to safety.

"Under the deck!" my dad yelled. We scrambled beneath the deck, pressing ourselves against the foundation of the cottage. Between the deck supports, we watched the approaching storm in silent terror.

The 200-foot-high waterspout shot toward us, not in the lazy way of a wave, but as if it had been fired from a cannon the size of the sun.

My dad shouted, "Hold on!" and something else I couldn't hear over the screaming wind. I think he was praying.

The spout sprinted over the final stretch of water, an animal eager to make the kill. It lunged over the crashing waves, it twisted through the blood-red sky, and then it hit the beach.

The waterspout literally skipped. And then like a monster of the night that is exposed to the sun, this monster of the water began to disintegrate when it hit land. By the time it reached our cottage, it was nothing more than a strong gust of water-colored wind that pelted our bodies. The rest of the storm raged for an hour and then simply blew away.

"Next time, we'll stay inland at Grandma's. Okay?" my dad said, tears of relief in his eyes.

We all agreed that would be a good idea.

Eliminating Clichés

Replace the following overused expressions, also known as clichés, with fresher ones.

Example: She fell head over heels in love with him.

Revised: In that moment as she looked at him, her heart radiated with warmth and she knew she was in love for the first time.

  1. Eat to your heart's content.

_____

  2. He heaved a sigh of relief.

_____

  3. I can hear you loud and clear.

_____

  4. There is more here than meets the eye.

_____

  5. I heard them laughing their heads off.

_____

  6. It was the last straw.

_____

  7. It was like looking for a needle in a haystack.

_____

  8. He felt it was a matter of life and death.

_____

  9. I was scared to death.

_____

10. Jack is as sick as a dog.

_____

Student Writing Sample

Vivid Description

1. *It was raining:* It was pouring down so hard that I could hear the rain drumming down on the sidewalk.

2. *John was tired:* John was practically asleep. As he was lying on the couch, his eyelids quickly closed and he didn't awake for a long time.

3. *It was cold:* I was about to freeze. I felt like I was in a pool of ice.

4. *A car drove by:* The bright red racing car zoomed by my eyes. I only saw it for a second!

5. *A cat sat at the window:* A big, fat, fluffy cat sat looking out my window. It saw a bird in a tall tree.

6. *It was hot:* It was 100 degrees outside and I could fry an egg on the sidewalk.

7. She felt nervous: As the girl was giving her speech, she was nervously shaking her legs.

8. *She looked beautiful:* Ms. America's sparkling gown glimmered in the spotlight as she walked gracefully on stage.

9. *The house stood empty:* The eerie, haunted house stood so silently empty that you could hear a pin drop. There was barely anything around.

—*Erin D.*

Imagery

Objective

The student will understand and use common literary devices to enhance writing.

Skills

—understanding the function and effect of simile and metaphor
—utilizing figurative language to enhance writing

Materials

—chalkboard
—student copies of "Figurative Language" (page 115)
—student copies of "Take a Dive into *Holes*" (page 114)
—writing paper
—student writing sample on page 116 (for teacher reference)

Procedure

1. First, write the following examples on the chalkboard:

   I was so nervous that my stomach felt like the Rose Bowl was being played inside it.

   My teacher, Mrs. Bellbottom, is like a snake in the grass waiting for me to pass a note to my friend Sam.

2. Ask students to identify the comparisons in both sentences. Ask students to explain how the comparisons are different.

3. Define and explain simile and metaphor to students. Similes are direct comparisons of two things, objects or people, using the words *like* or *as* or a word that functions as *like* or *as* in a sentence. Metaphors are direct comparisons of two things, objects, or people, without using *like* or *as* or any other qualifier.

4. Ask students to raise their hands to provide examples of both similes and metaphors. Write these on the chalkboard.

5. Review the following problems with similes and metaphors:

- **Triteness:**

  examples: He is a bonehead. She is a turkey.

  These expressions have been used so often that they have lost their power.

- **Inappropriateness:**

  example: The night was as dark as ink and the heavens were perspiring a cold sweat that blanketed everything.

  These comparisons are inappropriate because they do not help the reader visualize the desired image.

Imagery *(cont.)*

- **Mixed metaphors:**

  example: If the victorious allies had tried to put a fence around Japan and let her stew in her own juice, they would have created a festering sore.

  The mind cannot handle so many images at once. The writing loses its impact.

6. Distribute copies of "Figurative Language" to the students to complete.

7. Distribute copies of "Take a Dive into *Holes*" to the students. Ask students to identify the similes and metaphors in the article. Ask them to explain why the author chose to express his or her ideas using similes and metaphors.

8. Have each student write a paragraph in which he or she uses a simile or a metaphor to make his or her writing more vivid, alive, and interesting.

Publication

Collect the paragraphs and redistribute them to the class so that each student has a paragraph other than his or her own. Have the students underline the similes and metaphors they find in the paragraphs.

Extension

1. Bring in a collection of children's poems. Require students to find at least three examples of similes and metaphors in the poems.

2. Bring in a variety of pictures of interesting items. Display these around the classroom and ask each student to choose a picture and write a simile or a metaphor about it.

3. Ask students to bring in tapes or CDs of music that contain similes or metaphors.

4. Create a simile and metaphor wall in the classroom and require each student to contribute to it weekly.

Take a Dive into *Holes*

Poor Stanley. Not only has this overweight kid been picked on his whole life, but now he's been sent to a "bad boys" camp for a crime he didn't commit.

That's how *Holes* starts—and you might guess that the rest of the book would be pretty depressing. Well, it's not. Author Louis Sachar has included enough humor, action and surprising twists to keep you turning pages faster than you can shed a tear.

Our hero is a kid named Stanley Yelnats. (Get it? His last name is just his first name spelled backwards.) A hundred years ago, an old woman put a curse on the members of Stanley's family, dooming them to lives of bad luck and zero happiness.

Stanley is the perfect example of a curse working the way it is supposed to. His life has been one miserable episode after another. Now, he's been wrongly convicted of stealing a baseball celebrity's shoes. As punishment, he has to spend 18 months at a "camp" for juvenile delinquents in the middle of the desert. Each day, Stanley and the other "inmates" have to dig a hole five feet deep and five feet wide.

Why do they have to dig holes? The evil camp warden says it's to build character. But Stanley quickly realizes that the warden is using the other kids and him to search for buried treasure. And that's when the adventure really begins.

Stanley must escape the clutches of the warden and her henchmen, rescue a friend who wandered into the desert, discover the location of the hidden treasure, and free his family from the miserable curse that has haunted them for generations. All in all, a pretty major "to do" list.

The action in the book skips backward and forward in time. At first, it might be a bit tough navigating the waters of this swirling narrative. But once you get the hang of it, it's smooth sailing. The healthy doses of fantasy will also keep you from getting bogged down in the potentially depressing realities of the story.

Reading *Holes* is like shopping in one of those 40-acre superstores. You get a lot for a little. It doesn't take a lot of attention to stay hooked on this exciting book. And the author doesn't use a lot of extra words to provide an awesome story.

One downside: The dialogue—the way the characters talk—isn't always as natural as it should be. Often, the characters speak with the stiffness of cardboard cutouts. While this far from ruins the book, it might be a distraction to some readers.

I'm really not going out on a limb by giving this book a "thumbs up." *Holes* won the 1998 Newbery Medal for children's literature. This award is the Oscar of the young adult book world.

No, this book isn't rocket science. But it is an exciting adventure—with a plot that's full of holes. And I mean that in the best possible way.

Figurative Language

Vivid and interesting writing is often filled with figurative language, particularly similes and metaphors. These terms are not limited to poetry. Read the sports page in a newspaper and you will see a boxer described as *a limp octopus in the ring*. Notice the vivid images these figures of speech conjure up in your imagination. Popular songs also often contain figurative language.

Using complete sentences, write a simile for each situation.

1. you're exhausted

   _____

2. your back is sore

   _____

3. you're angry

   _____

4. you're happy

   _____

5. you're very strong

   _____

Now, using complete sentences, write a metaphor for each situation.

1. you're exhausted

   _____

2. your back is sore

   _____

3. you're angry

   _____

4. you're happy

   _____

5. you're very strong

   _____

Student Writing Sample

Simile and Metaphor

1. You're exhausted:
    I feel like a wet towel. I am a popped balloon.

2. Your back is sore:
    My back aches like I've been stabbed with a knife. My back is on fire.

3. You're angry:
    I am so mad I feel like a steam engine with the smoke puffing out my ears. I am a volcano about to erupt.

4. You're happy:
    My heart feels like its soaring in the air. I am a million tiny bubbles floating.

5. You're very strong:
    I am like an ox. I am Hercules.

—Katrina K.

Simile and Metaphor

About Allie C.:

    This person has a caring smile that shows kindness. She has hair that is as beautiful as the ocean's waves on a breezy day. This person's hands dance across the page as she writes so elegantly. Her art shows who she is and it is very, very good. She has a very good sense of humor and loves animals. This person is kind, caring, and joyful.

—Ashley N.

Rhythm

Objective

The student will identify and write sentences of various complexities and lengths to add style, energy, and emphasis to the writing.

Skills

—identifying and writing sentences that vary in complexity and length
—using fragments for effect

Materials

—student copies of "Back on the Chain Gang" (page 119)
—writing paper
—student writing sample on page 120 (for teacher reference)

Procedure

1. Distribute copies of "Back on the Chain Gang" to the students. Ask the students to use their pencils or pens to underline sentences that are particularly long and short in contrast to others.

2. Explain to students that writers vary the lengths of their sentences for a couple of reasons. First, providing a variety of sentence lengths prevents monotony and adds interest to the material. It also helps the reader to see what is very important. Short sentences stand out to most readers. Authors can also combine some ideas to make a sentence more complex.

3. Ask students to take a close look at the lengths of the sentences in the first paragraph.

4. Have them look at each of the six sentences separately. Ask them to characterize and analyze each sentence. For example, the first sentence is a short introductory sentence that establishes the topic and the tone of the article and it is followed by two longer, more complicated sentences that provide a great deal of information and detail. There are two more sentences that provide more information and detail that are neither short nor particularly long. The last sentence is a fragment as it is only two words. It leaves the reader feeling cut off and hanging on for more. It emphasizes that life on the chain gang is not easy.

5. Ask students to write paragraphs using the following information:

   Most dogs hate bathing. They have to be bathed. They fight having to be in a bath. Dogs have to be brushed. Soap and water are necessary for baths. Sometimes, they need a flea dip. After the bath, the dog smells better and looks better. The dog is softer to touch. The dog doesn't scratch or itch as much after a bath.

6. Have them use sentences of varying lengths to fulfill their purpose. They can add information, as needed.

Rhythm *(cont.)*

Publication

1. Have students share their paragraphs with a student in class. As each student reads his or her partner's paragraph, the student underlines the one sentence that stands out as the most important.

2. Allow students to read their paragraphs aloud to the class. As each student reads, ask the class to identify the sentence that stands out as the most important. Ask students to explain why.

Extension

1. Have students take a previously written essay and rewrite it using sentences of different lengths for effect.

2. Provide students with a variety of articles from newspapers and magazines in which the authors have deliberately used sentences of varying lengths for effect. Ask the students to find at least two examples of distinct sentence length changes and explain how it affects the essay overall.

118

Back on the Chain Gang

Alabama's first chain gang in decades does not yet know the drill. On a lonely stretch of highway near the Alabama-Tennessee border, guards and bloodhounds look on as some 320 convicts from the Limestone Correctional Facility try to negotiate the tricky business of walking in unison while shackled. Clad in immaculate white uniforms (emblazoned with the words "chain gang" lest anyone mistake them for pastry chefs), the men are equipped with a variety of tools and not quite sure whether they should be trimming, digging, or picking up litter. One makes a desultory attempt to start up a work song, but no one else joins in. Perhaps they're too busy looking forward to their lunch of bread smeared with jam. Perhaps not.

Chain gangs are meant to be unpleasant and this one is succeeding. "We don't like it," complains James Sears, convicted of harassment. "We think it's stupid." Civilians, on the other hand, seem fascinated by the sight of men in chains. Cars stop along the side of the road and mothers with babies get out to watch. A Limestone County school bus passes by and the children press their faces to the window.

Once a common sight along Southern highways, chain gangs fell victim to a reform movement that reached its zenith with the 1932 film *I Am a Fugitive from a Chain Gang.* By the late 1940s, the gangs were well on their way to joining stocks and public floggings in penological limbo. Thus there was little in the way of models when Alabama Governor Rob James decided last year to revive the practice. "We started from scratch," says Limestone warden Ralph Hooks.

In a single stroke, the gangs have fulfilled two of Governor James' dearest campaign promises: saving money (inmates, when chained, require fewer guards) and getting tough with criminals.

Fortunately, today's crews do not have to wear the heavy ankle irons that used to cause "shackle poison" (the new, handcuff-like shackles are made of lighter metals). Nor, in theory, will the men have to endure the overwork, beatings, and disease that led to death rates as high as 45% among "classic" chain gangs. Still, working on a '90s-style gang is not a picnic: inmates will be toiling through 12-hour workdays in the hot Alabama sun, serving sentences as long as 90 days. "If they try to escape," vows state corrections commissioner Ron Jones, "our officers are going to shoot them." No failure to communicate here.

Not everyone is pleased. The Alabama Civil Liberties Union is weighing a legal challenge, while some Alabama businessmen fear the gangs will hurt the state's image and sour its business climate. Out on the roadside, chain gang member Sears sees things in more elemental terms. "They won't allow you to chain five dogs together like this," he says with some anger. "We're moving backwards, not forwards."

Student Writing Sample

Dogs

A lot of people own dogs. We can tell by seeing people walking their dogs. Most kids look out the window of their car and say, "Oh, that dog is so cute," or they see a picture of a friend's dog. But, what dog lovers and owners find out themselves when they buy a dog is that dogs hate bathing even though they need to. A dog will do anything to get out of a bath. My grandma owns a dog and sometimes it seems like he knows he is going to get a bath or senses something is going on. I am amazed. After their bath, dogs need to be brushed. Sometimes besides a bath, dogs need a flea dip to get rid of the fleas they have. The dog smells a lot better and is softer to the touch after a bath and flea dip. They won't scratch or itch as much and everyone is happy.

—*Benjamin H.*

Sentence Variation

Objective

The student will use various sentence structures in order to provide interest and variety to the reader.

Skills

—using purposeful and varied sentence beginnings
—providing a variety of sentence structures
—constructing sentences that emphasize meaning

Materials

—student copies of "Latin Music Pops!" (page 123)
—writing paper
—printer paper
—student copies of "Joining Sentences" (page 124)
—brightly colored markers
—student writing sample on page 125 (for teacher reference)

Procedure

1. Distribute copies of "Latin Music Pops!" to the students. As the students read the article silently, ask them to identify at least four different sentence structures in the article. For example:

   —**Modifying clause, main clause:** Outside a Tower Records store in Manhattan, a chorus of screams is going up.

   —**Subject, modifying clause, verb:** The crowd of 5,000, mainly young women between the ages of Dawson's Creek and Felicity (with a few Rugrats and Ally McBeals mixed in), have gathered to catch a glimpse of the latest heart throb, their corazon.

   —**Main clause and main clause:** Ricky Martin is what is going on, and he's the center of something bigger than himself.

   —**Dependent clause, main clause:** Because Latin pop draws from different cultures, it also has the power to bring people together.

2. Write the following two sentences on the chalkboard:

   The boy sat on the hood of the car.

   The sun set over the ocean.

3. Ask the students to write five different sentences expressing the two ideas together. For example:

   —While the boy sat on the hood of the car, the sun set over the ocean.
   —The boy sat on the hood of the car and the sun set over the ocean.
   —The sun set over the ocean while the boy sat on the hood of the car.
   —Sitting on the hood of the car, the boy watched the sun set over the ocean.
   —The sun setting over the ocean shone on the boy sitting on the hood of the car.

Sentence Variation *(cont.)*

4. Divide the students into groups of three or four and provide them time to share their five sentences. The group will see how many different forms the two sentences generated.

5. Distribute copies of "Joining Sentences" to the students. Ask the students to try to develop the most interesting sentences possible.

Publication

Have each student tape together three sheets of printer paper. Assign each of the students one of the sentences from "Joining Sentences" and have them write their best sentence clearly and neatly on the paper using bold, dark colors. Post the sentences throughout the classroom.

Extension

1. Ask each student to rewrite a previously written essay to incorporate greater sentence variety.

2. Ask each student to bring in one example of published writing and identify at least five different types of sentence structures in it.

3. Provide students with short sentences for them to expand into longer sentences. For example, if the sentence is "The telephone rang," students can expand it to read, "The telephone rang with a shrill, demanding sound." Post the following sentences for expansion:

    —The lifeguard swam.

    —The computer turned on.

    —The girl screamed.

    —The detective ran.

    —The body fell.

    —The class shouted.

Latin Music Pops!

Outside a Tower Records store in Manhattan, a chorus of screams is going up. Mostly sopranos, a few altos, no tenors, and certainly no basses. "Riiiiiickyyyyyyyyyyyy! I love you!" The crowd of 5,000, mainly young women between the ages of Dawson's Creek and Felicity (with a few Rugrats and Ally McBeals mixed in), have gathered to catch a glimpse of the latest heart throb, their corazon. The fans at the front of the line enter the store and stumble out with a signature scrawled across a CD or on a poster or even on their skin. Some leave crying tears of joy. What's going on?

Ricky Martin is what's going on and he is the center of something bigger than himself. As a new century begins, a new generation of Latin artists, nurtured by Spanish radio, schooled in mainstream pop, are lifting their voices in English. Of this group, Martin, 27, is the hottest; Jennifer Lopez, 28, the most alluring; Marc Anthony, 29, the most artistic. With Hispanics poised to become America's largest minority group within the next few years, this music could be the sound of your future.

Because Latin pop draws from different cultures, it also has the power to bring people together. "Latino people have a golden key in their hands, a common treasure," says Colombian-born pop-rocker Shakira, 22. "That treasure is fusion. The fusion of rhythms, the fusion of ideas. We Latinos are a race of fusion and that is the music we make."

Some longtime aficionados even fear that the new pop Latin wave could wash away some very important cultural connections. Esmerelda Santiago, author of the memoir *When I Was Puerto Rican*, worries about the fact that the artists being promoted to superstardom mostly look Anglo, leaving the darker performers behind. "I'm sure that there are equally talented and gifted artists out there whose facial features don't conform as much to the European ideal."

Anthony has another concern. Although he knows Martin well and is good friends with Lopez, he is wary of media stories lumping them into a single group. "I don't know what they're talking about with this Latino crossover thing," he says. "I could see it if I was doing a salsa album in English. But you know what? We're not doing Latin music on English stuff. Latin-tinged, yes."

Trends come and go, stars wink and fade out. How long will this new crop hold out? "It's impossible to predict who will be a pop star forever," says Wayne Isaak, executive vice president of music and talent for VH1. "But (Martin, Anthony and Lopez) could have a longer career than most. Even if their pop following wanes a bit, they will always have this Latin fan base that can keep them playing Madison Square Garden and working with the best producers of the day."

And no doubt Latin music will continue to thrive all around the world as well.

Joining Sentences

A variety of sentence structures helps writing to have an easier flow for reading. It also helps to hold onto the reader's interest. Find five different ways to join the short sentences below in interesting and effective ways.

1. The scientist arrived at the crime scene. It was late at night.

_____

_____

_____

_____

_____

2. The sun beat down on Puerta Vallarta. It was drying the streets.

_____

_____

_____

_____

_____

3. Johnny dived to the side. He caught the ball.

_____

_____

_____

_____

_____

4. I studied all night before the test. I did not do well.

_____

_____

_____

_____

_____

Varied Sentences

1. **The scientist arrived at the crime scene. It was late at night.**

    It was late at night when the scientist arrived at the crime scene.

    The scientist arrived late at night to the crime scene.

    After the scientist arrived at the crime scene, he realized it was late at night.

    Late at night at the crime scene, the scientist arrived.

2. **The sun beat down on Puerta Vallarta. It was drying the streets.**

    When the sun beat down on Puerta Vallarta, it dried the streets.

    As the sun beat down on Puerta Vallarta, the streets dried.

    The streets dried as the sun beat down on Puerta Vallarta.

    The drying of the streets was caused by the beating sun in Puerta Vallarta.

    The beating sun of Puerta Vallarta dried the streets.

3. **Johnny dived to the side. He caught the ball.**

    Johnny dived to the side when he caught the ball.

    As Johnny caught the ball, he dived to the side.

    Diving to the side, Johnny caught the ball.

    After Johnny dived to the side, he caught the ball.

    Catching the ball caused Johnny to dive to the side.

4. **I studied all night before the test. I did not do well.**

    Even though I studied all night before the test, I did not do well.

    I did not do well because I studied all night before the test.

    I studied all night before the test, so I did not do well.

    Studying all night before the test caused me to not do well.

    All night before the test I studied, but I did not do well.

    Before the test I studied all night, yet I did not do well.

—Katrina K.

Alliteration and Assonance

Objective

The student will write with cadence to indicate that he or she has thought about the sounds of the words as well as the meaning.

Skills

—identify poetic devices in writing

—understand the effect of poetic devices in writing

—use the repetition of sound to reinforce or highlight important ideas

Materials

—chalkboard

—overhead transparency of "New Champs Take the Court" (page 129)

—overhead projector

—index cards

—marker

—large sheets of blank paper

—many newspapers and magazines

—scissors

—glue

—student writing sample on page 130 (for teacher reference)

Procedure

1. To introduce the concepts of *alliteration* and *assonance*, it is best to start with placing an example on the chalkboard for the class to see. Use the following example from the first line of Gerard Manley Hopkins' poem "As Kingfishers Catch Fire."

   As kingfishers catch fire, dragonflies draw flame/As tumbled over rim in roundy wells.

2. Ask the students to look, not at the meaning of the lines, but to look at the sounds of the words. Encourage them to identify any patterns of sound that they may see. They will probably notice that the letter *d* is repeated in *dragonflies* and *draw* (and also in *tumbled*). This is an example of *alliteration*, which is best defined as *the repetition of consonants* especially at the beginning of words. These words should appear very closely in writing in order for the sounds to be effective.

3. Next, they might notice the repetition of the *k* sound in *kingfishers* and *catch* and the *f* sound in *kingfishers*, *fire*, and *flame*. They may also hear the *r* sound in *rim* and *roundy*.

4. Place another example on the chalkboard. This is from Sylvia Plath's "Mushrooms."

   Our toes, our noses / take hold on the loam.

Alliteration and Assonance *(cont.)*

5. Students should notice the *o* sounds in these lines. *Assonance* can be a harder concept to teach. It can be defined as *the repetition of vowel sounds when the consonants are different.* For example, the *a* sound in *late* and *maid* or the *o* sound in *cold* and *foam*.

6. Ask students to think about why authors might use these devices in their writing. Ask them to think beyond, "Because it sounds pretty." Ultimately, repetition is used to highlight and reinforce ideas. Repetition of sound calls attention to the words and causes the reader to look more closely.

7. Display the overhead transparency of "New Champs on the Court" for the students to read.

8. Ask them to identify any use of alliteration or assonance in the article. Ask them also to explain what the use of these poetic devices has on the article.

9. Divide the students into groups of four and provide each group with a stack of index cards with the following words: *boat, ban, comb, fork, fat, load, dole, bed, spell.* Mix up the cards.

10. Have students work together in groups of three or four to organize the words in order to provide you with at least five examples of assonance and alliteration. Require examples of each.

11. Select groups to present their examples to the class. Place the examples on the chalkboard to reinforce the students' understanding of the concepts.

12. Have students work in groups of three or four to complete a poem using alliteration and assonance.

13. Instruct students to cut out fifty or more words (not individual letters to spell words) from newspapers and magazines. More words is better; the more students have to work with, the easier the assignment is to complete.

14. Encourage them to spread out the words, move them around, and play with them. Let them have fun and be silly. Have the students listen to the words they have chosen first, then work to use sound meaningfully, and finally try to find meaning in the words. Give them blank paper and glue so that they can lay their words out on the page. If they need additional words to fill in spots, have them return to the magazines and newspapers.

Alliteration and Assonance *(cont.)*

Publication

1. Allow the groups to read their poems aloud to the class. Have the rest of the class listen actively to identify the repetition of sounds.

2. Make a class book of the poems.

3. Display the poems on a bulletin board in your classroom.

Extension

1. Ask each student to bring in one example of each alliteration and assonance from literature or expository writing. Ask the students to explain how the author's use of the poetic devices affects the overall meaning of the writing. Place the examples on a bulletin board for the students to view.

2. Have each student write a paragraph or poem using alliteration and/or assonance to reinforce and contribute to the meaning.

New Champs Take the Court

Whack! A 114-mile-an-hour ball came hurtling over the net. Whack! Another one. Poor Martina Hingis! The Number 1 female tennis player in the world felt as if she were being "smacked."

After an intense battle on September, 11, 1999, Hingis finally surrendered and the U.S. Open had a new champion, 17-year-old Serena Williams. She became the first African-American woman to win the title since Althea Gibson in 1958.

The win was Serena's first singles title in one of the "Grand Slam" tournaments: the four biggest events in tennis. It was also sweet revenge. Her big sister Venus, 19, lost to Hingis in the 1997 U.S. Open finals and again in the semifinals match in 1999.

Powerful athletes with smashing serves, the sisters are ranked third (Venus) and fourth (Serena) in the tennis world. Though they compete against each other in singles, they are teammates in doubles. The pair is so close that some fans suggested Venus tired Hingis out so that her little sister could win! That's not true, but Serena says her sister's loss did inspire her to play better: "Venus was so bummed . . . That encouraged me to be even tougher out there.

Serena didn't have much time to celebrate her victory. "I had to go to sleep because I had another match," she said. The next day she and Venus won the U.S. Open women's doubles title.

What's more important to them—winning or sisterly love? "Tennis is a game; it's not your life," Serena says. "We really believe in family."

Student Writing Sample

Alliterative Writing

Brave beast began

Before the future generation dies

The evil guide does everything it can

To kill him.

—*Karen L.*

Alliterative Writing

Young black warrior

Born with rage

Wish for revolution

Search for democracy

Power to the people

—*James A.*

Spelling

Objective

Students will write frequently misspelled words correctly.

Skills

—using tactile experiences to practice spelling

Materials

—student copies of "The Federal Government Should Regulate Amusement Park Rides" (page 133)

—a list of frequently misspelled words for your students

—large pieces of paper

—crayons

—colored markers

—tempera paint

—paint brushes

—chalk

—chalkboard

—small sponges

—water

—dry erase markers

—white board

—glue

—pasta and/or popped popcorn

—masking tape

—pipe cleaners

—other art supplies

Procedure

1. Distribute student copies of "The Federal Government Should Regulate Amusement Park Rides." Ask the students to read the article and locate the misspelled words. Have them look for words that just don't look "right." Ask them to sound out words and to check the dictionary for correct spellings if necessary.

2. Review the correct spellings of words (*government, amusement, injuries, Jersey, accidentally, coincidence, association, fundamentally, involved, Illinois, automobile, thousands*). You may or may not wish to review spelling rules with students.

Spelling *(cont.)*

3. Provide students with a list of frequently misspelled words. (You can obtain these from vocabulary or grammar books.) Your list should include words your students use frequently in their speech and writing. Many books publish frequency lists, but not all lists will be appropriate for your students. Make sure to tailor the list to your students' needs. Some examples of frequently misspelled words are: *wastepaper, cupboard, environment, government, principal, embarrassment, burial, relieve, villain,* and *yawn.*

4. Provide students with many sheets of paper and assign the students a number of words (ten or more or as many as time will allow) to practice spelling from the list.

5. Have students write the words correctly using a variety of tactile experiences. Some may wish to use glue and pasta to spell the words, others may like to use a small wet sponge on a chalkboard covered in chalk to spell the words. The students may enjoy painting the words, using tape to spell the words, gluing pipe cleaners to paper, etc. By allowing the students to experiment with different tactile experiences, they may remember the spellings more vividly.

Publication

Display artist renderings of spelling words all over your classroom. If desired, stretch string along the middle of the classroom and use tape or clothespins to suspend the words from the string. Allowing students to look at the words regularly will help them to spell them correctly.

Extension

1. When students have completed a writing assignment, have them work in pairs to check for spelling. Have them search the paper for words that just don't look "right" to them or that seem incorrect when they sound them out. Give them dictionaries to use.

2. Create a word wall of frequently misspelled words in your classroom. Each time the students realize they are misspelling a word, they can write it on the wall in bold letters. This will help all of the students to spell that word correctly.

The Federal Goverment Should Regulate Amusement Park Rides

Recall the last time you rode on a roller coaster or other amusement park ride. Did you feel that shiver of fear that makes amusement park rides fun? Or did you have a deeper fear that you might be in real danger? In recent years, amusement park rides have caused several injurys and even deths. For example, in 1999, a roller coaster in Ocean City, New Jersy, acidentally rolled backward and crashed into another car. A woman and her 8-year-old daughter were killed in the accident. The federal government needs to create laws now that prevent tragic accidents like these.

Amusment park officials say that the increase in accidents is a sad concidence. Joel Cliff, spokesman for the International Assoceation of Amusement Parks and Attractions, said, "The Industry is fundimentally as safe as it has ever been." The association says that the chances of being killed on an amusement park ride are 1 in 250 million. However, if you or someone you love is invovled in one of these accidents, the odds make no difference.

The federal government does not regulate amusement park rides. Each state has different laws for amusement parks. One state, Illinoise, moved to inspect every roller coaster in the state after several accidents made news.

Think about all the regulations that make the food we eat and the water we drink safe. Think about all the laws that make automobil travel safer. No one wants to end the fun of amusement parks. Amusment parks are a favorite activity for thosands of families with children. Shouldn't the U.S. government try to protect them on roller coasters as well as in automobils?

Conjunctions

Objective

The student will use conjunctions to connect ideas.

Skills

—using conjunctions

—identifying using dependent and independent clauses

Materials

—student copies of "Latin Music Pops!" (page 123)

—writing paper

—student writing sample on page 136 (for teacher reference)

Procedure

1. Write the following coordinating conjunctions on the chalkboard: *and, or, for, so, nor, yet, but.* Inform students that these words are *coordinating conjunctions* when they are used to connect two main clauses. They are called coordinating conjunctions because they coordinate the ideas by giving them equal importance.

2. Provide the students with an example—***I** went to the store, and **I** bought gum.* In this example, both clauses are main clauses because they both contain a subject and a verb. In the sentence ***I** went to the store and bought gum,* the subject ***I*** is not present after the *and,* so it is not a main clause and no comma is needed.

3. Ask the students to write five sentences using these conjunctions to join two main clauses.

4. Review several examples with the class. Point out the use of a comma to separate the two clauses. When students join two main clauses with a conjunction, they must use a comma.

5. Write the following subordinating conjunctions on the chalkboard: *after, although, as, as if, as long as, as though, because, before, even though, how, if, in order that, once, provided that, rather than, since, so that, than, though, unless, until, when, whenever, where, wherever, whether, while* (sometimes *who* and *which*). Inform students that these words are subordinating conjunctions when they are used to connect one main clause and one dependent clause. The more important idea is placed in the main clause so that it can stand alone. The less important clause is placed into a subordinate section that can never stand alone because it is dependent on the main clause.

Conjunctions *(cont.)*

6. Write the following sentences on the chalkboard, and ask students to identify the independent and dependent clauses:

   • Although Mike is tired, he is still watching television.

   • I have to work until the kitchen is cleaned.

   • I studied all night even though I know the material well.

   • Jack won't cooperate unless you give him gum.

   • Before I can go to bed, I have to do my homework.

   • When I go skating, I have to wear a helmet.

7. Ask students to write five sentences using subordinating conjunctions to join their ideas.

8. Review several examples with the class. Carefully review the punctuation of each student example.

9. Distribute copies of "Latin Music Pops!" to the students. Ask them to identify sentences using either coordinating or subordinating conjunctions by underlining them.

Publication

1. After reviewing sentences in class, ask students to rewrite ten sentences, making sure that the punctuation is correct. Collect the sentences for assessment.

2. Ask each student to select one sentence from the activity and turn it into a well-developed paragraph or essay.

3. Have each student write a paragraph or essay using at least two sentences containing conjunctions. Encourage them to use one of each—coordination and subordination—in order to vary the sentence structures.

Extension

1. Have a poster-making contest in the class. Ask students to work in groups to make informative posters about conjunctions. Some groups should make posters for coordinating conjunctions and some groups should make posters for subordinating conjunctions. Prominently display the finished posters in the classroom as models for the students.

2. Require students to find two examples of subordination or coordination in sentences by looking through textbooks. Have them write down their examples and share them with other students in the class.

Student Writing Sample

The Keeping Room

   In the beginning of the story . . . I feel proud that my father is going into battle. Although I fear for him and would rather that he stay at home, I am very pleased that my father is in charge of troops and that he will be leading them into battle. I want to be just like Father; brave, strong, kind, firm, and a leader. Therefore, I share his opinions and strive to act like him.
   I do not believe that I'm ready to be the man of the house, but I vow to do whatever it takes to protect my family. I wish to be important. Without Father here I feel inferior, which, I suppose, I am.
   When I do my studies with Euven, I feel cooped up. I wish to be out in the fields, leaping and yelling. Although I want to be educated, I would much rather be fighting in battle than learning Shakespeare. Oh, well. I will probably soon be proving myself worthy because it is said that the British are soon to invade our town. Then I will fight like a man, and people will look up to me as I look up to Father.

—Hannah B.

Paragraphing

Objective

The student will organize information in distinct paragraphs to signal new ideas.

Skills

—organizing information using paragraphs

—maintaining only one main idea in a paragraph

Materials

—student copies of "Get Some Sleep in the Deep" (page 139)

—textbooks (any kind except math)

—student copies of "Monumental Battle" (page 140)

—writing paper

—student writing sample on page 141 (for teacher reference)

Procedure

1. Distribute student copies of "Get Some Sleep in the Deep." As students take turns reading portions of the article aloud to the class, ask them to look at the paragraphing. What causes the writer to begin a new paragraph? What is the main idea of each paragraph? Paragraphing for expository writing is very different than for narrative writing, but the principles and rules remain the same.

2. Explain to the students that while some may be tempted to write essays with no paragraphs, paragraphing is very important in writing because it signals to the reader that the writer is moving on to a new idea. Inform students that only one main idea belongs in a paragraph and when the author moves on to a new main idea, he or she begins a new paragraph.

3. Ask the students to look through textbooks to identify exact places when writers begin new paragraphs.

4. Distribute copies of "Monumental Battle" to the students. Divide the students into groups of two or three and inform them that this is a real article, but the paragraph breaks have been removed. It is their job to determine where the paragraph breaks belong. They may do so by using a "_" where they believe the paragraph should begin. (Paragraphs begin at: "Natural beauty is . . . ," "History is etched . . . ," "It is also a land . . . ," "In September 1996, . . . ," "After the President . . . . ," and "The Clinton Administration . . . .")

5. Have each student write a defense on writing paper of his or her paragraph decisions. The student must have an explanation for each paragraph break.

6. Inform the students that they will be chosen randomly to present their decisions to the class at a later time and they must defend their choices by explaining how the main idea changed.

Paragraphing *(cont.)*

Publication

1. Have students take their copies of "Monumental Battle" and their written explanations home to have them reviewed by their parents or guardians. Encourage them to practice their oral explanations with their families.

2. Place the copies of "Monumental Battle" and the written explanations on a bulletin board for the class to review.

Extension

1. Ask each student to write a narrative essay in which he or she describes a place he or she has visited. The student should write in such a way that the reader will want to visit it, too. Encourage the student to use many details to entice the reader to the location. The place might be a local restaurant, a park, or it might be an exotic vacation spot. Inform the student that you will be looking very closely at the use of paragraph breaks to signal a new main idea when you read the essay.

2. Require each student to find one article or excerpt of writing from a book or magazine. Have the student write an explanation of each paragraph break in the selection of writing. When the student brings the article and explanation to class, have him or her exchange assignments with a classmate and carefully review his or her work.

Get Some Sleep in the Deep

Over 130 years ago, author Jules Verne first dreamed up the idea of humans living underwater. In *20,000 Leagues Under the Sea*, Verne describes a crazy captain who lives underwater for years in a futuristic submarine.

In 1870, people thought Verne and his idea of underwater living were crazy! But his vision of the future turned out to be pretty accurate. Today submarines don't seem strange at all.

Still, even Jules Verne might be surprised by an amazing hotel in Key Largo, Florida, that bears his name. At the Jules' Undersea Lodge, guests don't just get to see tropical fish in a saltwater lagoon—they also get to sleep with them!

The lodge, which is located 21 feet underwater, has two bedrooms, a bathroom, and a living room. Giant round windows allow guests to peer out onto an endless parade of sea creatures. Schools of angelfish, parrotfish, and barracuda peer back at the humans inside the hotel!

The Undersea Lodge was originally built as a scientific laboratory for ocean research. NASA used it to explore the similarities between life underwater and life in outer space.

In 1986, the lodge was redesigned as the world's only underwater hotel. Guests, who pay $325 a night, arrive in diving suits and enter through a small pool and air lock. Once inside, they breathe normally. They can even watch TV and order underwater room service!

At night, escaping air creates soft bubbling sounds that are ideal for slumber. Says lodge worker Rick Ford: "Most people say it's one of the best night's sleep they've ever had."

Would Jules enjoy a stay at his namesake hotel? "I think so," says Ford. "It holds true to his dream of living in the ocean in comfort."

Monumental Battle

Natural beauty is more valuable than coal. History is etched into the striped sandstone canyons of the Grand Staircase–Escalante National Monument in southern Utah. The Grand Staircase began forming 250 million years ago, as colliding landmasses lifted the Colorado Plateau while rivers dug into it. It is, says environmentalist Ken Rait, "a land of outstanding beauty." It is also a land at the heart of a battle that pits environmentalists and the U.S. government against many of Utah's residents. For years people have fought over the fate of these 1.7 million acres. Some people want to use the land instead of protecting it. They say that locked in the area's rocks are as much as 62 billion tons of coal, plus valuable oil and natural gas. They add that mining coal from just one site in the area could mean a $3 billion profit for Utah. An additional $1 billion in coal profits would flow into the state's school systems. However, mining would destroy one of the most magnificent spots in America. Fortunately, the U.S. government has taken steps to protect the area's natural beauty. In September 1996, President Bill Clinton signed an order that made this huge stretch of Utah a national monument. Tourists and locals can continue to use the area for hunting, camping, and grazing. But mining is discouraged. After the president signed the order, shops and schools near the monument closed in protest. Many people in that area believe Utah's economy needs the jobs and money that mining brings in. Some Utahns have been building roads across the protected lands. Under the law, land that is already developed and in use is freed from some federal protection. While these people's anger may be understandable, their reaction is short-sighted. Once destroyed, the natural beauty of the area can never be recreated. When the coal, oil, and gas are gone, as they inevitably will be, what then? The Utahns should consider how the land's beauty might serve their interests better than mining in the long run. Tourists coming to see the Grand Staircase would prove to be a stronger and longer-lasting source of income for the local economy than mining ever would. The Clinton Administration is sticking to its decision to protect the monument. Soon after Clinton's order was signed, however, federal officials met with local leaders in Utah to find ways to protect the local economy as well. Interior Secretary Bruce Babbit has said, "We want to live together out there." Involving area residents is an excellent idea. Hopefully with the federal government's help they will come to see that what is above ground is more valuable than what is below.

Student Writing Sample

Identifying Paragraph Breaks

1. ¶–in between "...outstanding beauty" and "It is also a land..." because the writer changes from writing about what it looks like to the battle about it.

2. ¶–in between "...magnificent spots in America" and "Fortunately, the U.S...." because the writer goes from talking about why they should mine the land to how the government is protecting it.

3. ¶–in between "But mining is discouraged" and "After the president..." because one paragraph is about how the land is a national monument and is protected, and the next paragraph is about how the people are mad and how they are fighting it.

4. ¶–in between "...freed some federal protection" and "While these people's anger..." because the next paragraph is about what is going to happen to the land if they mine it. How it will be ruined by mining.

5. ¶–in between "...what then?" and "The Utahns should consider..." because instead of talking about how the mining is going to ruin the land the writer talks about how the people should have tourists come.

6. ¶–in between "...than mining ever would" and "The Clinton Administration..." because that new paragraph is about how they are trying to compromise.

—Rebecca M.

The Dash and Colon

Objectives

The student will correctly use a dash in writing to emphasize ideas.

The student will correctly use a colon in writing to emphasize ideas.

Skills

—understanding the use of a dash

—using a dash in writing

—understanding the use of a colon

—using a colon in writing

Materials

—student copies of "The Snap Decision" (page 144)

—writing paper

—chalkboard

—printer paper (three sheets per student)

—clear tape

—student writing sample on page 145 (for teacher reference)

Procedure

1. Distribute student copies of "The Snap Decision." Ask students to attempt to define how the dash is used in a sentence based on the examples in the article.

2. After students have presented their definitions, inform them that a dash is used to signal a dramatic pause in writing. The author uses a single dash to emphasize what follows. The dash is slightly stronger than the comma in creating a pause.

3. Take time to look at several of the examples in the article and review the grammatical structure of each sentence.

4. Ask the students to look for the use of a colon in the article. Like the dash, it is used to direct attention to the material that follows an opening statement. The colon is stronger than the dash in formal writing. The colon joins two complete sentences when the second sentence is to be strongly emphasized.

The Dash and Colon *(cont.)*

5. Other examples of the colon in writing are as follows:

   • to signal a list:

     I need the following groceries: apples, carrots, and lettuce.

   • after the opening of a formal letter:

   Dear Sir:

   • when telling time:

     It is 10:00 a.m.

6. Ask students to write four sentences—two using the dash and two using the colon—on their own sheets of paper.

Publication

1. Allow some students to write their sentences on the chalkboard. If you find a mistake, be sure to use it as a teaching opportunity and review the error and how to correct it with the entire class.

2. Type up all of the dash sentences and colon sentences on separate sheets of paper and duplicate them for the entire class to keep in their notebooks and use as models in their own writing.

Extension

1. Ask students to make educational posters for the classroom about the dash and the colon. Require them to provide original examples and clear definitions.

2. Provide students with a variety of reading materials. Have them find two examples of both the dash and the colon in their reading. Ask them to write down the examples and place all of the examples in class books.

3. Have each student tape together three sheets of printer paper. Have each student write one sentence using a dash or a colon on the paper using brightly colored markers. Display the model sentences prominently in your classroom.

The Snap Decision

Pokémon Snap is a game with a lot of shooting. You shoot as you float down the river, you shoot as you drift on the winds from a dark cave, and you shoot everything in sight as you hover over the sands of a tropical beach. What makes this video game different? You're not using a weapon to shoot—you're using a camera.

That's right. You're a photographer who visits Pokémon Island for the ultimate photo shoot. Your mission: to take the best photos of the 150 wild Pokémon that wander the island.

Sound kind of strange? It is. Sound easy? It's not. These wild Pokémon—like Pikachu, Snorlax, and Sandshrew—have not been tamed and have minds of heir own. Some pop up for just a split second. You have to be extremely fast with your camera if you want to get a decent shot. Plus, your vehicle is constantly cruising down 3D "courses," giving you limited time.

What's that I hear? A groan of horror at the appearance of yet another product spawned by the Pokémon craze? Save that groan for the Backstreet Boys' salt and pepper shakers. Pokémon Snap is different. This time you're not trapping the Pokémon or forcing them to fight. You're just taking their pictures as they frolic in their zany way about the island.

Unfortunately, this island feels very small. If you've ever played Banjo Kazooie or even Mario Kart, then you know that the power of Nintendo 64 allows game designers to create gigantic worlds. They can give players endless levels and infinite options.

Too bad the designers of Snap didn't follow these examples. They've created an island that will leave players feeling claustrophobic. After only two hours, I had explored the entire island—and was already getting bored.

Sure, there are a few secret passageways, but the limited number of "courses" is made worse by the fact that you can't control how you travel through them. Like the old-fashioned cars at Disneyland, your slow vehicle is stuck on a secured track. Yes, you can use the C buttons to look around, but you can't control the direction of the movement—and that will frustrate many players.

What's good about the game? For years, kids have been saying that video games help teach basic life skills. But unless your basic life includes plans to travel to Saturn to battle alien cyborgs who want to eat human brains, this argument hasn't carried much weight.

Snap changes all that. It shows you how to compose—or put together—a decent photograph. A character named Professor Oak takes a look at your photos and judges them based on elements such as the pose of your Pokémon. Your Snap photos might not make it on the cover of a magazine, but you'll learn a few fundamentals of photography.

In short, this game provides a nice, gentle vacation from the typical action-packed experience, plus it provides tips on taking good photos. But the small island, the limited number of courses, and the repetitive action might bore players. They might want to pack their bags and go home!

Student Writing Sample

Using Dashes and Colons

1. My favorite colors are: blue, green, and turquoise.

2. She's great at tennis: she's the best.

3. I went to school—like I always do—by walking.

4. Lizzie Maguire—that show on Disney—is my favorite.

—Cameron J.

The Semicolon

Objective

The student will correctly and effectively use a semicolon in writing.

Skills

—using a semicolon correctly and effectively in writing

Materials

—student copies of "What is a Hero?" (page 147)
—chalkboard
—student writing sample on page 148 (for teacher reference)

Procedure

1. Instruct students about the use of the semicolon in writing. It is used to separate main clauses within a sentence, but it also connects two sentences that are very closely related. The semicolon indicates a longer pause and a stronger emphasis than does a comma in writing.

2. Show students that the semicolon is used in two situations:

   • to connect two complete sentences: He did not go to school today; he is very sick.

   • in a series between items that contain commas: The Olympic skiers were from: Butte, Montana; Seattle, Washington; and Nantes, France.

3. Distribute copies of "What is a Hero?" to the students. Allow students to choose partners and ask them to read the article. Have the students find examples of the use of the semicolon in the article.

4. Have students write the examples on the chalkboard for the class to see.

5. Instruct the partners to write five sentences using semicolons. Sometimes a semicolon cannot be used to effectively join two sentences.

6. Ask each of the members of the group to choose their favorite sentence with a semicolon and write a paragraph in which it is used.

Publication

Create a class book of the semicolon paragraphs. Keep the book in your class library as a reference book for students.

Extension

In a future writing assignment, require each student to use at least one sentence with a semicolon.

What Is a Hero?

How do ordinary people define a hero? To find out, *LIFE* magazine asked its readers which of five admirable traits they felt was most important in a hero. Forty-six percent of the readers said "being honest" was the most important. This trait far outpaced "changing society for the better" (19 percent); "having courage" (11 percent); "overcoming adversity" (11 percent); and "being a leader" (10 percent).

By these standards, everybody has it in his or her capacity to be heroic in the eyes of a neighbor, each and every day. But many of the eternal greats—the Lincolns, the Washingtons, and beyond—possessed them all.

That's the impression *LIFE*'s editors got after they heard some well-known people discuss heroism. Together, these personal views paint an intriguing, often poignant picture of humanity at its best. Which of the views do you share?

Robert Fagles, translator of Homer, the Greek author of *The Odyssey: Hero* in Greek means warrior, but it's anyone who struggles. They're men and women of words and action, both. Heroes exist to dwarf us; they're models we aspire to.

Howard Zinn, historian: There's a heroism in artists and entertainers who make a lot of money and yet refuse to stick to that. (The comedian) Dick Gregory was one, and (the poet) Allen Ginsberg was another, and (the folksinger) Pete Seeger.

Bill Gilbert, Tecumseh biographer: Two cultures that produced large numbers of principled heroes are the North American Indians and the ancient Greeks. A central purpose of these societies was producing heroes. Obtaining honor, wealth and power were secondary.

Fred Rogers, host, *Mister Rogers' Neighborhood*: As a hero, I think of a person who has a disability but who treats each day as a gift.

Sissela Bok, professor, Harvard University: John McCain crashed in Vietnam. His arms were broken, his leg mangled. He was a prisoner for years. When he came out, he was asked, "How did it feel when you heard Americans were protesting the war?" He said, "I thought that's what we were fighting for—the right to protest." What McCain did in Vietnam was heroic.

John McCain, U.S. Senator (R-Ariz.): I have seen people confronted with crisis act in a way that is almost divinely inspired. In prison, I saw men rise to levels of heroism in their ability to overcome pain. . . . I was honored to be in their company.

Anthony Lewis, *New York Times* columnist: A Supreme Court hero, I think, was Justice Hugo Black in the middle of this century. He was relentless, committed. He was the great believer in First Amendment liberty. He used to say, "When they wrote that Congress shall make no law abridging the freedom of speech or of the press, they meant no law, none at all!"

Bob Kerrey, former U.S. Senator from Nebraska and Medal of Honor recipient: A hero loves, and in love acts upon the belief that someone's life is more important than his or her own. A hero is not made of stone: A hero fails, doubts, cries and suffers despair. A hero loves and is loved in return.

Student Writing Sample

Christmas at Grandma's House

One Christmas when I went to my grandma's house with my family, almost everyone on my mom's side of the family was there. When it was time to open presents, I noticed that every one of my presents from my grandpa had special wrapping paper and a little pen shaped like an elf. Also my sister had a little Winnie the Pooh with her presents; she loves Winnie the Pooh. At the end of the time I had received nine little pens and an assortment of different outfits.

—Elena C.

Capitals

Objective

The student will use capital letters properly in writing.

Skills

—using capital letters properly in writing

Materials

—student copies of "Blazing a Twisted Trail" (page 151)

—sheets of paper

—poster board

—markers

—student writing sample on page 152 (for teacher reference)

Procedure

1. Distribute copies of "Blazing a Twisted Trail" to the students.

2. Place the students into groups of two and ask them to read the article together.

3. Have the students identify the different uses for capital letters in the article. Each group should write these down on a sheet of paper. (See below.)

   - as part of a title
   - proper noun: names of persons
   - proper noun: countries, nationalities, races, languages
   - at the beginning of a sentence
   - proper noun: states, regions, localities, and other geographical divisions
   - proper noun: organizations and their members

4. Ask the groups to identify the capital letters one at a time and review the rule behind each capital letter. When completed, ask students to add to the list other rules for capitalizing. These might include the following:

   - the beginning of a sentence
   - the first word of each line of poetry (sometimes, not always)
   - the first word of some fragments
   - the first word of a direct quotation
   - the first word of a formal question
   - oceans, lakes, mountains, deserts, streets, avenues, parks, routes
   - educational institutions, schools, departments, courses
   - corporations, governmental agencies or departments, trade names
   - calendar references (holidays, holy days, days of the week, months)
   - the word *I*
   - abbreviations after names

Capitals *(cont.)*

5. As students work to develop the list, encourage them to look through their textbooks, reading materials, the newspaper, and other resources to find ways that capital letters are used.

6. Review all of the rules and examples as a class. Have the students take notes.

7. Ask each student to write a paragraph or an essay in which he or she uses at least seven words that require capital letters. Have the student write the essay without capitalizing the words so that he or she can give the paper to a classmate to find the words that should be capitalized. Each student should identify the reason the word needs capitalization, as well. Encourage the students to incorporate some of the less common reasons to capitalize in their paragraphs.

Publication

1. Have the students use poster board and markers to make educational posters about capitalization for the classroom in which they develop original examples. Assign one type of capital letter to each student.

2. Place the corrected paragraphs from above in a class book for your classroom's reference library.

Extension

Provide students with a variety of written materials in which you have not capitalized words. Have students work to identify the words in need of capitalization. Have them identify the reason for capitalization as well. The students should label each place in which capitalization is needed with colored markers and explain their reasons in the margins.

Blazing a Twisted Trail

Adrian Fisher is a-maze-ing! The Englishman is a professional maze designer. He creates walk-through mazes that people must solve by finding a clear path from entrance to exit.

In 1996, Fisher, 44, broke a record by making the largest maze ever. The Michigan corn maze, in the shape of a car, contained more than three miles of pathways between rows of corn plants! At least 2,000 people could hunt their way through it at once.

"People like corn mazes," Fisher told *TIME For Kids*. "They're entertaining, out in the sunshine and open air." He has been building mazes for more than 20 years and has built at least 135 of them so far. His specialty is setting up tricky roadblocks, including fountains, mirrors, and even tanks of live crocodiles and fish!

One of Fisher's favorites is a Beatles maze in England, which includes a 51-foot-long yellow submarine. He has also made colorful mazes for school playgrounds.

"Eleven- and twelve-year-old children are often better than their parents at navigating a maze," Fisher says. "Grown-ups get a bit stuffy."

Do any grown-ups take a professional puzzlemaker seriously? You bet. The Norton Museum of Art in Florida opened an exhibition of Fisher's work in January 1997. Fisher is not at all surprised. "Maze design is very much like art," says the great maze master. "There's a story behind each one."

Student Writing Sample

My Mom

A lot of people are special to other people. Truly, my mom is special to me. My mom is special because she takes care of me when I am sick. Also, she is there when I am hurt. Out of all the people in the world, no one can replace my mom.

One thing about my mom is she loves ice cream. In addition to ice cream, my mom loves sherbet and yogurt. My mom's favorite thing to do is bike because she loves to get out and do things. Truly, my mom's favorite color is green because both of us have green eyes. Also, my mom has brown hair, green eyes, and tanned skin.

One of my mom's favorite places to visit is New York. After all, her family lived and grew up there. My mom was born on December 5, 1959. Throughout my mom's early years, her mom curled her hair every day. Of course, my grandma also curled my mom's five sisters' hair, too. My grandma died when my mom was in her teen years due to cancer.

Throughout my mom's middle years, she went to high school and college. When my mom finished college, she began working at a place called Qualcomm. My mom really loves Qualcomm because it is a great place to work, plus there are many nice people to work with.

Throughout my mom's late years she got married to my dad. That is also when my mom had me. In fact, when I was six, she had my brothers.

Truly, I love my mom because she takes care of me when I am sick, is there when I am hurt, plus gets me nice things. To repeat, no one in the world can replace my mom.

—Elenor B.

Completeness/ Comprehensiveness

Objective

The student will edit and revise manuscripts to improve the meaning and focus of writing by adding, deleting, consolidating, clarifying, and rearranging words and sentences.

Skills

—editing written material

—revising written material

Materials

—overhead transparency of "Jackie Robinson's Greatness" (page 155)

—overhead projector

—student copies of "Evaluation and Revision Form" (page 156)

—colored marking pens

—dictionaries and thesauri

—student writing sample on page 157 (for teacher reference)

Procedure

1. Display the overhead transparency of "Jackie Robinson's Greatness" for the class to read.

2. When you finish the article, review the elements of a finished, completed piece of writing, as is evidenced in the article about Jackie Robinson. For example, the author uses a strong hook in the introduction of the article to draw the reader in. The author most likely added details (like the exact date Jackie Robinson played professional baseball for the first time) after he wrote his first draft. The author may have deleted information that was unnecessary to achieve the goal of his essay (perhaps there was a paragraph about Jackie Robinson's marriage). The author most likely consolidated information so that the topic of paragraph three is about the challenges he faced when he began playing professional baseball. The writer may have had to clarify information in the fourth paragraph because some readers may not understand what a "level playing field" is. The writer surely had to rearrange words and sentences in his final draft so that the essay is readable and powerful. For example, his sentences about Michael Jordan are very well-constructed and use powerful words like *curt* and *violated* in a persuasive way. The essay also concludes very effectively because it sums up the contents of the article, but also brings the reader full circle.

3. Begin by explaining to students that the final product of writing that we read in newspapers, magazines, and books is produced after a long and difficult process of drafting, revising, and editing. It is very helpful to have an outsider's view of our writing because the reader is better able to see the areas where the writer is not clear or where the writer lacks needed information. The best way to accomplish this is through read-around groups or writing workshops.

Completeness/ Comprehensiveness *(cont.)*

4. Have each student select a piece of his or her writing that has not been revised or edited. Ask them to make three copies of the writing for the workshop. In addition, select the topics you want students to address in their writing workshops. For example, you may want the students to look closely at titles or at the use of quotations. First provide a brief lesson on the topic, then instruct students to review and edit each others' papers focusing only on that topic. This process can extend over a period of days or weeks, depending on how many topics you wish to focus on with your students. You can also use the general revising and editing form found on page 156 with students as a final revising and editing review.

5. Place the students into groups of four. Distribute colored marking pens to each student and provide a dictionary and thesaurus to each group.

6. Distribute three copies of "Evaluation and Revision Form" to each of the students. The students will be reading, evaluating, and making revision recommendations for three papers other than their own.

7. Once students have completed their read-around group work, provide them enough time to discuss the essays.

8. Have students complete their final, polished drafts.

Publication

Produce a class newspaper or newsletter in which you publish the essays. Send it to other classrooms or home to parents.

Extension

Provide all students with an early draft of an essay and make an overhead transparency of it. As a class, determine the elements the students should examine in the essay as they edit and revise it. Ask them to edit and revise the essay.

Jackie Robinson's Greatness

I wish I could really remember the time in 1950 when my dad took me to Ebbetts Field to see Jackie Robinson play for the Brooklyn Dodgers. But I was only three years old and the day is a blur. No matter, my dad explained to me many years later, he wanted me to be in the presence of history.

How quickly we forget. Fifty years after Robinson broke the color line in major league baseball, far too many people, both black and white, fail to understand the significance of his achievement.

When Robinson took the field with the Dodgers for the first time on April 12, 1947, America was wallowing in apartheid. Clearly, Robinson was the best candidate to step over the color line that divided America. At 28, with World War II service in the Army behind him, Robinson was mature and tough enough to withstand the taunts of racist fans and opposing players. And he was, literally, an All-American—in football at UCLA. Moreover, Robinson understood everything that was riding on the experiment. He left his natural combativeness in the locker room and endured incredible abuse without fighting back. He let his batting and base-running speak for him—and they spoke eloquently.

There is a reason why so many black men have tried to follow in Robinson's footsteps, pouring all their ambitions into the hope of a career as a pro athlete. Sport is one of the few arenas of American society in which the playing field is really level. If you get across the finish line first, you win. If you're as good as Robinson was, your acclaim transcends racial boundaries. But unless you get a chance to compete, you can never demonstrate your ability.

Robinson had the guts to speak out against racial injustice after he retired from baseball. In 1963, he traveled to Birmingham to be with Martin Luther King Jr. after four little black girls were blown to bits in the bombing of a church. "The answer for the Negro is to be found, not in segregation or separation, but by his insistence upon moving into his rightful place, the same place as that of any other American within our society," he argued.

You can hardly imagine contemporary black sports superstars taking an equally brave stand on a divisive moral issue. Most are far too concerned with raking in endorsement dollars to risk any controversy. Recently Michael Jordan brushed off questions about whether Nike, which pays him $20 million a year in endorsement fees, was violating standards of decency by paying Indonesian workers only 30 cents a day. His curt comment: "My job with Nike is to endorse the product. Their job is to be up on that."

On the baseball field or off it, when Robinson came up to the plate, he took his best shot and knocked it out of the park. The superstar athletes who have taken his place, sadly, often strike out.

Evaluation and Revision Form

Name of the writer: _____

Date written: _____

Name of the reader: _____

Date read: _____

Title: _____

What is the title of the essay? _____

Can you suggest another title for the writer? _____

_____

Introduction:

Does the writer have an interesting hook to grab your attention? Explain. _____

_____

What is the organizational structure? _____

_____

Body:

What are some of the many details and examples to support the writer's ideas? _____

_____

Name the best detail or example. _____

_____

Name the weakest detail or example. _____

Is there anything the writer should clarify? _____

Is anything confusing in the essay? _____

Make a suggestion: _____

Transitions:

Identify some of the transitions in the essay. _____

Name some of the transitions the author uses to link the paragraphs together._____

Is there sufficient unity in the essay? _____

Conclusion:

Sum up the writer's argument. _____

_____

How could the writer make the essay come full-circle? _____

In addition to looking at the content of the essay, you also need to examine the spelling, grammar, syntax, and punctuation of the essay for the writer. Any corrections you have should go directly on the essay.

Student Writing Sample

The Keeping Room

    In the beginning of the book, *The Keeping Room,* I feel really sad that my husband is leaving for war. I'm scared for him and afraid that he will die. Later on I feel a bit better, but I am still extremely scared and hoping that my husband will come home. I am scared, but I try to hide it in front of my children so that they won't worry too much.

    I go on with my life as usual and try not to think about him leaving, but sometimes I can't help it. I hope that he doesn't die in the war and he comes back with a victory. Hopefully, all will go well and my husband doesn't die.

—*Jessica Y.* (writer) and *Hannah B.* (editor)

Page Layout

Objective

The student will present his or her writing in a manner that enhances the reader's ability to understand and identify with the ideas.

Skills

—integrating text and visuals

—using visuals to support and point out important textual information

Materials

—overhead transparency of "On the Brink" (page 160)

—overhead projector

—several magazines with color pictures

—scissors

—glue

—paper

—student writing sample on page 161 (for teacher reference)

Procedure

1. Display the overhead transparency of "On the Brink." Ask students to observe how the animals are arranged on the page, in what direction they are facing, and the size they are (full body or cropped to show just part of them).

2. Point out to the students that the way the pictures of the animals are arranged on the page deeply affects how we, the viewers, react to them.

   • The pictures are clean, crisp, realistic illustrations of animals.
   • All pictures are close up, which makes the picture more intimate.
   • Each picture attempts to capture the unique characteristics of the animal.
   • The pictures are arranged on the page as a rectangular frame that surrounds the text.
   • Each animal is facing either the text itself or is looking at the reader.

3. Have the students select a variety of pictures from magazines. Inform them that they will be selecting pictures that support and point out the important elements of their writing. They will need to find elements in the photos themselves that unify all the pictures together in a theme. For example, how the picture was taken, in what direction the subject is looking, the colors used in the photos, the angle used to take the picture, the distance between the photographer and the subject in the photo, etc.

Page Layout *(cont.)*

4. After they select their pictures, the students will need to determine how they want to lay out the pictures on their pages. They may wish to work with partners to decide what will work best for their pictures. They should ask themselves the following:

   • Will the pictures frame the text?
   • Will the pictures appear in the middle of the page or line the top or sides?

5. Ask the students to consider the positions that are most pleasing to a viewer.

6. Once the layout is complete, students should complete the writing portion of the assignment.

Publication

1. Have the students meet in groups of four to present their brief essays and collages. Make sure each student has an opportunity to discuss his or her design decisions.

2. Have the students meet in groups of four to identify how the pictures are unified and how the pictures support and point out the important elements of the writing. Place the pages and the student explanations in a class reference book for the library in your classroom.

3. Display the essays in your school library.

Extension

1. Provide students with a number of examples in which an author uses many photos to support his or her main ideas in a piece of writing. Ask each student to select one of the examples and write an explanation of how the photos support the writer's important points. Ask the student how the layout reinforces the writer's ideas.

2. Give the students time to search the Internet for a variety of layout techniques. Have the students present their findings to the class. (In order to ensure student safety, be sure to monitor all Internet use.)

On the Brink

mandrinette
status: critically endangered

Philippine eagle
status: critically endangered

sea otter
status: endangered

fossa
status: endangered

common sawfish
status: critically endangered

Iberian lynx
status: endangered

Will these species disappear?

Take a close look at the species on this page. It may be the last time you see them. Scientists have long warned that animals and plants are disappearing at an alarming rate. But the crisis may be even worse than everybody feared. That news comes from the IUCN Red List, an assessment of the health of the remaining species. (IUCN stands for the International Union for Conservation of Nature and Natural Resources.) Of the 18,276 organisms investigated, 11,046 are threatened with extinction. That number includes 24% of all mammals and 12% of all birds.

The outlook for certain groups is especially grim. The number of critically endangered primates has risen 50% in four years, largely as a result of habitat loss and the demand for "bush meat." The number of critically endangered freshwater turtles, prized in Southeast Asia for food and medicines, has more than doubled. Among birds, the number of threatened albatross species jumped from three to 16, owed to long-line fishing. Even more alarming, say environmentalists, is that the Red List comprises just a fraction of the world's 1.75 million known species—let alone the millions more that have yet to be discovered.

The IUCN categorizes threatened species in three categories: critically endangered, endangered, and vulnerable. For rough definitions of each group, see the key.

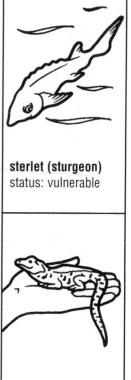

sterlet (sturgeon)
status: vulnerable

Chinese alligator
status: critically endangered

CRITICALLY ENDANGERED: faces extremely high risk of extinction in the wild (not necessarily in zoos) in the immediate future; numbers have been reduced at least 80% over the past 10 years.

ENDANGERED: faces a very high risk of extinction in the wild in the near future; numbers have been reduced at least 50% over the past 10 years.

VULNERABLE: faces a high risk of extinction in the wild in the medium-term future; reduction of at least 20% over the past 10 years.

Asian three-striped box turtle
status: critically endangered

wandering albatross
status: vulnerable

Having Diabetes

I am diabetic so I am not allowed to eat certain foods. But everywhere I go I am tempted by sweets and candy. All of my friends can eat chocolate chip cookies with their lunches or they go buy chocolate kisses. The only sweets I can eat safely without causing problems with my blood sugar is fruit, and I even have to watch how much I eat of them. I like strawberries, but I like them with whipped cream. And my mom makes a great lemon pie without the meringue. Having diabetes is hard, but it's okay if you know what to eat.

—Jeff B.

Graphs and Charts

Objective

The student will present writing in a manner that enhances the reader's ability to understand and identify with the ideas.

Skills

—developing questions for an investigation

—brainstorming a topic

—integrating text and visuals

—using visuals to support and point out important textual information

Materials

—overhead transparency of "How Kids Feel" (page 164)

—overhead projector

—graph paper

—white paper

—colored markers or pencils

—poster board

—glue

—student writing sample on page 165 (for teacher reference)

Procedure

1. Display the overhead transparency of "How Kids Feel" and have students look at the bar graphs and pie charts as you read the text.

2. Divide the students into groups of three and discuss the results in the graphs and charts on the page.

   • Would these statistics have a different affect on the reader if they were presented textually?

   • The author does comment on the results of question one in the introduction, but the rest of the questions are left without commentary. Why?

3. Ask the students to brainstorm different topics with their groups that they could use in a poll. For example, what are the qualities of a good friend, a good teacher, a good pet?

4. After they have chosen their topic, have them develop at least three different questions and conduct the polls in class. They can then organize their results in bar graphs or pie charts (or both) using the graph paper, plain white paper, and colored markers or pencils.

5. Ask students to design posters to express their main ideas and the results of their polls. Remind them to consider their layouts carefully and to use color to help focus the reader's attention on what is most important.

Graphs and Charts *(cont.)*

Publication

1. Display the posters throughout the classroom, in the school office, in the school library, in the cafeteria, etc. (Sometimes the district office is in need of student work to decorate the walls. When students know that their work will be posted in public places outside of the classroom, the quality of work is often better.)

2. Take digital photos of each of the posters to make a digital photo gallery. These can be incorporated into your class Web site for parents and family to see. (Be sure to obtain the necessary permission before displaying student work on the Internet.)

Extension

1. Take students to the library to locate two examples of media in which the author has used graphs or charts to enhance writing material. Ask the students to show their examples to the class and discuss their findings.

2. Invite students to locate Web sites that contain polling information. For example, *www.gallup.com* is the Web site for the Gallup Organization. Have the students select polling results from a Web site, present the results visually, and write a paragraph discussing the results. (Be sure to monitor all Internet use in order to ensure student safety.)

How Kids Feel

From mid-May through June 1, 1999, researchers sat down in shopping malls with 1,172 kids, ages 6 to 14, in 25 U.S. cities. Their goal: discovering how kids felt about their lives. The poll was taken for Nickelodeon, the TV channel, and TIME magazine. Kids from a sample designed to match the entire population of kids in the U.S. were interviewed one-on-one and without their parents. Pollsters also interviewed 397 parents.

What emerged loud and clear from the study is that kids are very happy to be kids and they don't view the world as the nasty place their parents view it to be. Nine out of 10 say they feel safe in many schools and neighborhoods. While parents list crime, violence and guns as the worst aspects of being a child today, kids don't. "Getting bossed around" and having to do homework and chores are far more pressing issues for kids. None of the bar graphs add to exactly 100% because respondents were asked to choose more than one item.

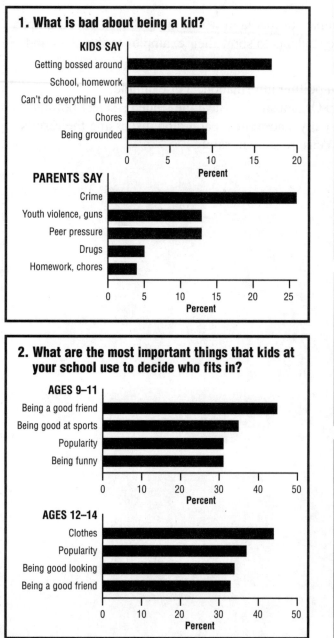

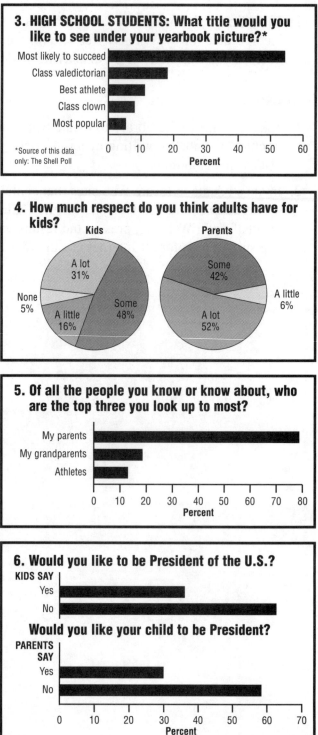

Student Writing Sample

Do You Do Too Much Homework?

After taking a poll of twenty students in the fifth grade, I know that kids feel like they have too much homework. Only one student said he thought the amount of homework was fair. Most kids are spending two hours on homework a night. They say that two hours is hard to do every night because they don't have time to play sports, games, practice the piano, or watch TV. They say they have to spend half their time doing math homework, which is boring because it is the same thing over and over. Some kids think they can learn just as much by doing only half the problems. Maybe the teachers need to give less homework.

—Kate N.

Maps and Diagrams

Objective

The student will present writing in a manner that enhances the reader's ability to understand and identify with the ideas.

Skills

—integrating text and visuals

—labeling a visual to aid the reader's understanding

—using visuals to support and point out important textual information

Materials

—overhead transparency of "Invasion of the Nanoprobes" (page 168)

—overhead projector

—science books or library books

—paper

—colored pencils or markers

—writing paper

—student writing sample on page 169 (for teacher reference)

Procedure

1. Display the overhead transparency of "Invasion of the Nanoprobes." Ask the students to examine the diagram as you read the article aloud.

2. Have the students pair up and ask them to discuss the benefits of using a diagram with this particular subject.

   • Does the diagram help the reader to understand the written material?

   • Would the reader have trouble visualizing a nanoprobe if there were no image in the article?

   • What is most helpful about the diagram: the pictures or the captions?

3. Ask the students to look at the way the captions are worded. Do they notice, for example, that all of the items identified are described using parallel structure?

4. Have some of the groups present their opinions about diagrams and captions with the class.

5. Ask the students to look in science books or library books to find topics about which to diagram and write about.

6. You might want to choose a topic so that the students are working around a particular theme or you might even have students diagram a sentence or a paragraph, identifying the elements they have studied and know. Students could also diagram a telephone, computer, or other object they use or have studied.

Maps and Diagrams *(cont.)*

7. Have them make the diagram to show what the subject looks like and how it works.

8. Make sure they use captions and encourage them to use the visual to enhance the reader's ability to understand their written material.

Publication

1. Display the diagrams on a bulletin board in your classroom. Have the students spend time evaluating them and require them to write about their favorite diagram.

2. Place the diagrams in a class book. Have some of the students prepare the binding of the cover for the book. Display the book prominently in your classroom or put it in your class library for easy reference.

3. Display the diagrams in your school library, the principal's office, the district office, or in other public places at your school.

Extension

Take a trip to the library. Ask students to locate and copy two examples of diagrams and summaries of the textual material they support from sources in the library. Ask students to bring these to class and exchange them with a partner. Encourage students to look at the way the material is presented visually and how the captions are worded.

Invasion of the Nanoprobes

Robots as tiny as germs may one day prevent and cure a host of diseases.

Imagine an army of tiny robots, each no bigger than a bacterium, swimming through your bloodstream. One platoon takes continuous readings of blood pressure in different parts of your body; another monitors the waxy buildup of cholesterol; still others measure blood sugar, hormone levels, developing arterial blockages, and immune-system activity.

Such are the dreams of the nanotechnologists, engineers at universities like M.I.T., Princeton, and Carnegie Mellon, who are already redefining the meaning of the word miniature. The prefix of *nano*- refers to a billionth part of a unit—the size range these visionaries are talking about. Already, nanotechnologists have built gears and rotors far thinner than a human hair and tiny molecular "motors" only 50 atoms long.

But that's just the beginning. Within a few decades, nanotechnologists predict, they will be creating machines that can do just about anything, as long as it's small. Germ-size robots will not just measure internal vital signs. They will also organize the data with molecular microcomputers and broadcast the results to a mainframe computer (implanted under your skin, perhaps), where the data can be analyzed for signs of disease. Nanomachines could then be sent to scour the arteries clean of dangerous plaque buildup, or aid the immune system in mopping up stray cancer cells, or even á la *Fantastic Voyage,* vaporize blood clots with tiny lasers.

If the nanotech guys are right, a call to the family doctor a few decades from now could yield a high-tech variation on an old cliché: "Take two teaspoons of diagnostic sensors, and call me in the morning."

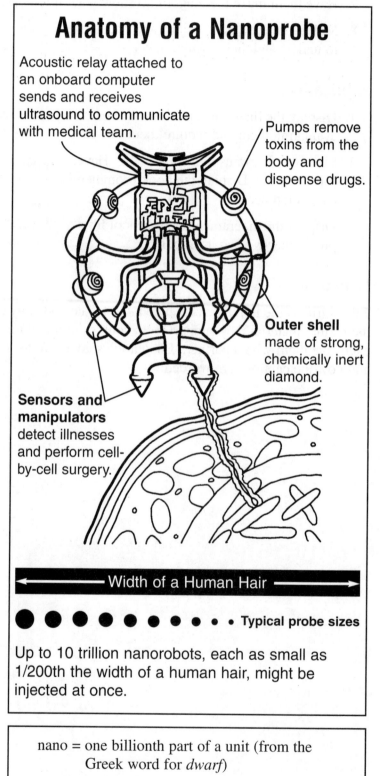

Anatomy of a Nanoprobe

Acoustic relay attached to an onboard computer sends and receives ultrasound to communicate with medical team.

Pumps remove toxins from the body and dispense drugs.

Outer shell made of strong, chemically inert diamond.

Sensors and manipulators detect illnesses and perform cell-by-cell surgery.

← Width of a Human Hair →

● ● ● ● ● ● • • • **Typical probe sizes**

Up to 10 trillion nanorobots, each as small as 1/200th the width of a human hair, might be injected at once.

nano = one billionth part of a unit (from the Greek word for *dwarf*)

probe = a medical device used to explore parts of the body (from the Latin word for *examination*)

Teeth

Did you know you get two separate sets of teeth in your lifetime? It's true! Between four months and three years you get your first set of teeth, called the milk or deciduous (which means they fall out) teeth; ten in the lower jaw and ten in the upper jaw. You get two incisors, one canine, and two molars on each side of both jaws. But when you are about six years old, your baby teeth fall out because your permanent teeth come in. There are more permanent teeth: 32 in all.

—Kyle L.

Diagram 1

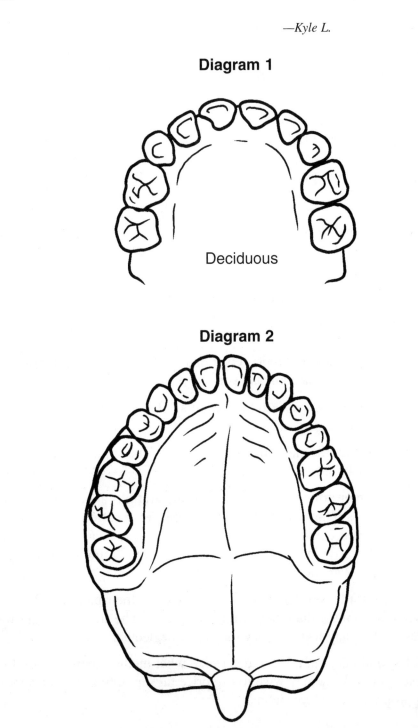

Deciduous

Diagram 2

Permanent

Photos and Illustrations

Objective

The student will present his or her writing in a manner that enhances the reader's ability to understand and identify with the ideas.

Skills

—brainstorming

—integrating text and visuals

—using visuals to support and point out important textual information

Materials

—overhead transparency of "Sports Overload?" (page 172)

—overhead projector

—student copies of "Photos and Labels" (page 173)

—photos or illustrations

—large sheets of white construction paper

—markers

—glue

—student writing sample on page 174 (for teacher reference)

Procedure

1. Display the overhead transparency of "Sports Overload?" As you read the article to the class, ask students to examine the photo that accompanies it.

2. Distribute copies of "Photos and Labels" to the students. Have them complete the activity while working independently or with a partner.

3. Review the students' work with the class to ensure that all of the students understand the purpose and effect of using photos with labels.

4. Ask the students to produce or bring to class photos or illustrations about a particular subject. These may be a picture of a sibling, an illustration of a teacher, a cartoon of a coach, and so on. They may also choose to feature items like a refrigerator, a couch, a car, etc. You may wish the students to use a theme. For example, all people who work at the school, all different types of people involved in the Civil War, etc.

5. Have the students brainstorm lists of features they can label on their pictures. They should produce lists that are much longer than they will actually use. The students might want to check with partners in class to find any features they may have neglected.

6. The students should also brainstorm a list to determine what method they will use for labeling their photos or illustrations. They may wish to use price tags, pointing fingers, sports equipment, pencils, or other appropriate and clever items.

Photos and Illustrations *(cont.)*

7. At this point, students should be able to write the text of their articles. They will be writing about topics of their choice, but they will be using their photo or illustration to deepen the reader's understanding of their main points. For example, if the writer has chosen a coach as a topic, perhaps he or she will write about how students need to listen to their coaches more because they are more than just P.E. teachers. The student can label the coach's caring eyes, ears good for listening, mouth good for advice-giving and guidance, arms good for hugging, etc.

8. Have students mount their photos or illustrations on large sheets of construction paper so that they can easily label them with markers.

9. Students should post their articles on the large paper as well.

Publication

1. Have the students share their photos or illustrations and text in groups of four. Have the groups choose which student's work is the best and present that one to the entire class.

2. Post all of the photos or illustrations and the text throughout your classroom. Students will get creative ideas from seeing the work of their classmates.

3. Create a big book of the assignments. Take the big book to another classroom to share with another class.

Extension

1. Use the editorial section of the newspaper in your classroom for a period of time. Have students read the political cartoons and look to see how the topics addressed in the opinion section correspond with the subject of the political cartoon.

2. Have students look through newspapers and magazines to examine how photos are used to support and enhance the content of the newspaper articles. Require them to find examples of powerful and effective photos or illustrations and their accompanying text.

Sports Overload?

The amount of time and money families spend on sports is soaring.

Kelly Donnelly plays soccer. Boy, does she play soccer! Not long ago, the New Jersey teen spent all weekend on the soccer field—three games on Saturday and three on Sunday.

Sound familiar? America's soccer and baseball fields, hockey rinks, and basketball courts are filled with kids kicking, swinging, skating, and dribbling. Forty million American kids play organized sports. But it's not just the number of kids playing that's amazing. The amount of money and time parents are investing in kids' athletic careers is soaring out of the ballpark! Kelly's parents will pay about $3,000 this year for her soccer expenses including club dues, private clinics, summer camps, and travel.

Many parents pay top dollar so their kids can have the best private lessons and equipment. Others spend hours driving their kids to games. Has America's love of competition gone too far? Or are the benefits of team sports worth the huge costs and intense pressure to win?

Some experts say kids benefit from playing team sports as long as they are having fun. "We know from a lot of research that kids who participate in sports tend to do better academically," says Mark Goldstein, a psychologist at Roosevelt University in Chicago, Illinois. "It forces them to be more organized with their lives."

Pushy parents and insensitive coaches can take all the fun out of playing. Many say that's why 73% of kids quit their sports by age 13. "They stop playing because it ceases to be fun and pressures put on them by coaches and parents don't make it worthwhile," says Fred Engh, a professional coach and author of the book *Why Johnny Hates Sports*.

Even worse, physical injuries from intense competition seem to be

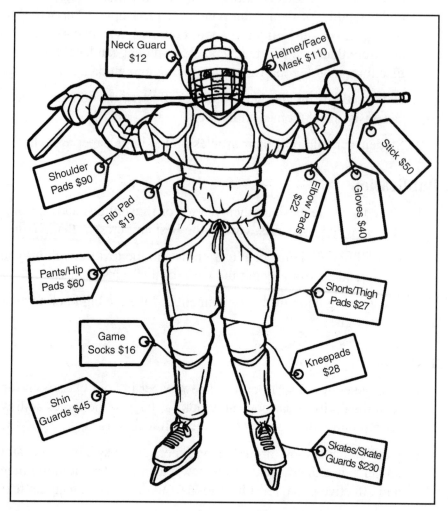

on the rise. Roughly 4 million kids between ages 6 and 16 end up in hospital emergency rooms for sports-related injuries each year, the Consumer Products Safety Commission reports. Eight million more are treated for medical problems caused by athletics.

Some parents hope their kids' athletic skills will win them college scholarship money. This hardly seems realistic, though, since fewer than 1% of the kids playing sports today will qualify for a college athletic scholarship.

The critics sound like a bunch of sore losers to families that live for sports. They say the joy of sports can't be measured in dollars and cents—or runs and goals. "It's my

life," says Aidan Wolfe, 10, who plays soccer in Portland, Oregon. "I love soccer. If my parents told me I couldn't play anymore, I'd be devastated."

The Right Stuff

Ice hockey is the most expensive of the team sports. It takes a lot of cold, hard cash to suit up for a game. The boy above, age 10, wears all the necessary gear. Total cost: $749.

Photos and Labels

1. Does the photo help you to understand the article?

    _____

2. Is the photo clever or humorous? Explain.

    _____

    _____

3. Is the photo creative or artistic? Explain.

    _____

    _____

4. How is the subject featured? Is he looking to the left, right, or at the reader? How does this affect how we perceive him?

    _____

    _____

    _____

5. What does the author emphasize by labeling the hockey player's gear with price tags?

    _____

    _____

6. What is the effect of showing a hockey player in full gear instead of just listing the different items and their prices?

    _____

    _____

    _____

Kids That Are Forced With Major Responsibility

Many children are forced to take on adult roles in life. For example, Joseph Kershaw, the main character in Anna Myers' *The Keeping Room*, is forced to take on his father's role while his father is away fighting in the Revolutionary War.

I think Joseph's role of protecting the family and house is an overwhelming task. Joseph is hesitating over the idea of taking over his father's place. Joseph doesn't know if he can take over a colonel's job at the mere age of 12.

The picture to the right contains symbols representing Joseph's life. For example, the pole Joseph is carrying represents the responsibility Joseph is placed with. On one side of the pole there is a family and a musket; the family represents Joseph's family and the musket represents the Revolutionary War. On the other side of the pole there is a house and an American and British flag. The house is representing Joseph's house, and the flags are representing the two countries at war. The giant footsteps in front of Joseph are representing Joseph trying to follow his father's footsteps. The giant shadow behind Joseph is representing the man Joseph is trying to be.

—David M.

Answer Key

Page 21

I. Means of Transportation

  A. Automobiles

    1. cars

    2. trucks

    3. sports cars

      a. Ferraris

  B. Airplanes

    1. jets

      a. Stealth bombers

    2. Cesnas

  C. Trains

    1. electric trains

      a. bullet trains

      b. trolley

  D. Boats

    1. yachts

    2. cruise ships

      a. the Titanic

I. Clothing

  A. Footwear

    1. sneakers

    2. sandals

      a. flip-flops

  B. Caps

    1. berets

    2. baseball hats

  C. Pants

    1. jeans

    2. shorts

    3. slacks

  D. Shirts

  E. Suits

Page 81

Negative words:

gigantic

opinionated

hovel

weak

stubborn

skinny

used

messy

tacky

old

strict

inspector

tyrant

companion or bosom buddy

stubborn

frigid

devour

short

cut back

nosy

old

pungent

Page 133

amusment	(amusement)
injurys	(injuries)
deths	(deaths)
acidentally	(accidentally)
amusment	(amusement)
assoceation	(association)
fundimentally	(fundamentally)
Illinoise	(Illinois)
automobil	(automobile)
amusment	(amusement)
thosands	(thousands)
automobils	(automobiles)

Skills Matrix